GROW

25 SIMPLE STEPS TO BUILDING A PROFITABLE ONLINE BUSINESS

GROW

TRIM

JOE BRITTON

FOUNDER OF #4 FASTEST GROWING COMPANY IN AMERICA *DELOITTE

GROW, GROW, TRIM
25 Simple Steps To Building A
Profitable Online Business

Copyright © 2018 Joe Britton

Published by Today Is The Day Publishing
www.todayisthedaybook.com

ISBN: 978-0-692-08245-4
Printed in the United States of America

For more information or to reach the author, go to:

www.GrowGrowTrim.com

ACKNOWLEDGMENTS

I wanted to personally say thank you to the following people for their support and the role they played in making this happen: Elza Sofie, Jon Brantz, Ross Greenberg, Geoff Gross, Glen Abbott, Mort Greenberg, Burton Breznick, Brian Mast, Eyal Lichtmann, my brothers Evan and Matt Britton, Mom, Dad, Irene, and my son Logan Luca Britton.

Secrets from a former Yahoo and Amazon employee, founder of the 4th fastest growing company in America.
— Ranked by Deloitte

CONTENTS

INTRODUCTION

"Being aware of your fear is smart.
Overcoming it is a mark of
a successful person."
— Seth Godin

Don't Settle For Another Person's Dream

So you want to be an internet entrepreneur? You've come to the right place. You may be reading this book on your lunch break or after a long day at work because you want more out of your life. Maybe you bought this book because you're tired of running on the corporate treadmill. Maybe you bought it because you're yearning to "live your dream" in a world where a lot of talented, hard-working people live in fear of losing their job.

What if I told you there is a freer way of living out there in the digital realm?

What if I told you the impossible *is possible*?

Back when our grandparents were starting out, the entrepreneurial opportunities were limited to "real life" – but now we live in this amazing time where any one person can go online and literally change the world. It doesn't matter what college you went to, or where you live, you can turn your great idea into a moneymaking internet venture that will allow you to quit your day job.

I am a living testament that it can be done.

A few years ago, I was just like you. I wanted to be successful. I had dreams of owning my own internet business but I had no idea where to start. All I knew was I had all these great ideas, a passion for technology and didn't want to work for "the man."

I spent many sleepless nights mulling the question every entrepreneur asks him or herself: *How am I going to pay my bills while I get this idea off the ground?* This question is one of biggest setbacks stopping entrepreneurs from pursuing their life passions.

Don't fall for it. It's a trap.

I know way too many smart people who are paralyzed by fear, paralyzed by their credit card debt or their mortgage. They have great ideas but have convinced themselves that they can't afford to quit their jobs – so they do nothing about their dreams and keep coasting through their lives.

If you feel like you are trapped in a job you "can't live without" – the reality is *you are living in a gilded cage you built for yourself. The only bars keeping you down are imaginary.* The job security you think you have is only an illusion.

Do you want to know what real job security looks like?
Be your own boss.
Don't settle for someone else's dream.
Chase yours.
It's not too late. Every passing minute is another chance to turn it all around.

Belief Is The Antidote To Fear

If the only thing preventing you from following your dreams is the fear of losing that steady paycheck – what if I told you that you can actually earn more money on your own than you're earning at your current job?

This may sound like a pipedream but it's true.

Over the next 150 pages, I will teach you 25 essential steps you can utilize to build your very own internet start-up business that makes money. I want to show you that there are a lot of amazingly easy ways to earn money online, some which take little, to no effort, at all on your part.

Let the internet work for you.

Just promise me one thing: Don't put this book down until you've read it cover-to-cover. I want to be in your ear until you believe what I'm saying. That's not too much to ask, look at the size of this thing! It's not like I'm asking you to plow through *Moby Dick*. Come on, what else do you have to do with your day, post another Instagram picture of your food?

Take this ride with me; it'll be painless and highly educational.

Don't you want to live the life you know you deserve? I know you do.

The first step to changing your life is to believe in yourself and your ability to succeed. Haven't you heard? *Belief is the antidote to fear.*

All the great entrepreneurs have the "fearless gene," so dig deep and find it within yourself. Then use it as a weapon.

And if you can't find it inside of you, *fake it till you make it*. Whenever the dogs of doubt start nipping at your heels (and they will), tell yourself, "If I believe it, then it's true." Whenever the haters say it can't be done, say, "Tell it to someone else because (say it with me now...) if I believe it, then it's true."

Make it your mantra.

If you can overcome your fear of the unknown, you've already won half the battle. Instead of desperately clinging to a job you don't love, you will suddenly wake up and realize you don't want to waste your life working on someone else's dream.

It's time to start fulfilling yours.

You Have To Take Huge Risks To Achieve Great Things

Who am I anyway? I'm definitely not your average Joe.

I'm an energetic tech entrepreneur with over 20 years of experience who started three successful internet companies that have earned more than $50 million dollars in revenue.

I'm really proud of the fact that I currently run *SearchMarketers.com*, which *INC Magazine* and *Deloitte Fast 500* recently ranked as the "4th fastest growing company in the United States".

Let me tell you, my success didn't happen overnight. I had to "cut my teeth" working for three technology companies you may be familiar with (*Ask Jeeves, Yahoo* and *Amazon*) before I set out on my own. I thought I was living the dream working for these companies but after a few years I noticed I had some pretty cool ideas for internet businesses of my own.

Did I really want to look up in 20 years and realize I've been working on somebody else's dream my entire life?

Sure, the benefits were amazing and they all were "cool" places to work – but I decided I wanted to do something amazing so I pushed all my chips into the middle of the table and bet on myself.

It was a gutsy move. My friends and parents thought I was totally insane – but I left those high paying tech jobs and never looked back. I believed in myself (and my dreams) even when I wasn't exactly sure what those dreams were!

You have to take huge risks to achieve great things.

And I did. Some of my internet start-ups were hits while others were busts, but that's just the nature of the boom or bust business. I'm just as proud of my internet startup failures as I am of my "hits." Why? Because every failure taught me lessons I never would have learned if I had not experienced them myself.

Even in defeat (and I experienced plenty), I didn't give up. I knew there was something special out there for me so I remained committed to my quest to find greatness in the world, and in myself.

Find Creative Ways To Stand Above The Crowd

I knew what greatness looked like in the flesh. I had my first brush with it when I was in college. It was my senior year at the University of Maryland, I understood one way to learn how to be great is to listen to other successful people.

Around this time, it just so happened that a friend gave me an extra ticket to see President Bill Clinton speak on campus. I grabbed the opportunity. It was a sold out event. President Clinton was in the middle of being accused of some scandalous activity at the White House but I wasn't so concerned with his personal life. I was immediately struck by his presence. He was (and still is) an amazing speaker.

I learned a lot from his speech that day but then something really serendipitous happened after the presentation. While everyone was giving him a standing ovation, I decided to walk up to the front and introduce myself. I was nervous but my gut said, "Just go up there and see what happens," so I did.

I let adrenaline guide me through my fear.

As I got closer to the podium, I noticed the entire auditorium was thinking the same thing! A big crowd formed behind me. Now I was just a face among thousands. How could I stand out?

I looked down and saw an open chair right in front of me – impulsively I hopped up on it and suddenly I was two feet taller than anyone else.

Just then, President Clinton walked down to greet us, and the crowd went nuts. Something inspired me to yell, "Mister President! It's a damn pleasure to meet you!"

What happened next?

President Clinton walked right up to me and gave me

a high five. He said, "Thank you very much, sir!" The crowd went wild. I was in shock.

Later that day, I told all my friends about meeting the President but no one believed me. Until a few days later, when *The New York Times* published a picture of Bill Clinton and me on the cover, no less.

I couldn't believe I was on the front page of *The New York Times* with the President of the United States! I know high fiving the President is not some huge achievement but having a photo of the exact moment when I was able to overcome my "fear" was a big deal to me.

You have to understand, in college I could talk a good game but (like a lot of people in this world) I was still a kid inside who had fear of failing, fear of saying the wrong thing, fear of being rejected. Not anymore.

This moment gave me confidence to keep following my gut and not be afraid of falling on your face. This is one of the greatest traits an entrepreneur can have in this world!

I credit President Clinton with helping me beat my fear. From that moment on, I knew that if I wanted to end up on the front page again – I had to channel my uncertainty, follow my gut and keep finding ways to get noticed in the crowd, again and again.

Cutting My Teeth @ Ask Jeeves

That's not to say I completely erased fear from my vocabulary. After I graduated from the University of Maryland, I was paralyzed with fear just like everyone else.

How was I going to fare out in the real world?

I had no idea but I kept listening to my gut and channeling my anxiety. I moved to New York City, of all places. I didn't know what I was going to do with myself but I knew it was going to be something amazing.

I moved into a new place in Manhattan. It was great (sort of). Actually it wasn't all that great but I had a great attitude so I didn't mind! I lived in a partitioned part of my brother's kitchen for three years! I paid rent for my half of the kitchen and only requested that our other roommates avoid using the microwave early in the morning or late at night (since the sound woke me up.) They listened *sometimes* – other times, I didn't care.

I was on a mission to get my first amazing job!

As fate would have it, my positive energy attracted a positive outcome.

My brother introduced me to a guy named Mort Greenberg who offered me a job at *AskJeeves.com*. If you're too young to remember, *AskJeeves* was a search engine built to compete with *Google* that had a butler character named "Jeeves" that you could ask any question to. It was kind of a precursor to Apple's Siri but with no voice.

AskJeeves seemed like a great company so I was super excited to begin work. The *AskJeeves* search engine fascinated me. I began to study it. After looking at thousands and thousands of the top search queries, I realized that as much as the internet is full of people looking for flights, mortgages or products – there are even more web surfers out there who are looking for pictures, videos or games.

This was a revelation.

I spent the next five years at *AskJeeves* helping them grow from a small private company into a hot publicly traded company on the NASDAQ, which sold for two billion dollars to *IAC* (Interactive-Corp), a company owned by business mogul, Barry Diller (you may have heard of him).

While I was still at *Ask Jeeves*, IAC merged us with three other web companies (*Excite*, *Iwon.com*, and *Max Online*, one of the first performance ad networks.) I couldn't believe it. Three years into my professional career and I was suddenly working for Barry Diller!

At *IAC*, I was able to learn a whole different side of the internet that I didn't know existed. I learned about the world of "sweepstakes and promotions" from an *IAC* website called *Iwon.com* that would (one day) inspire me to start my own company that combined the search engine technology of *Ask Jeeves* with an "*Iwon*-like' sweepstakes.

I called my idea *SearchChips.com* and it was the first company to offer rewards and prizes to consumers for simply searching the web.

I thought I was on to something big.

Working On The Next Big Thing

Even though my body was working for "the man," my entrepreneurial mind was always working on my big dream. I knew the next big thing was somewhere *out there* just waiting to be discovered by somebody – *why couldn't it be me?*

My teammates over at *iWon* were getting millions of hits just from people trying to win cash & prizes from a sweepstakes; wouldn't that work in other web incarnations?

Could a search engine that gave away stuff be the next big thing? I mean, who was even making a website like this?

I did my homework; the answer was nobody. I had already seen how much money search engines make when users click on paid ads at *AskJeeves;* I felt my idea was even better. I called my concept a "search engine rewards" site.

The idea was pretty simple. Do you know how credit card companies give away rewards to people who use their credit cards? *Searchchips.com* worked the same way. Every search on our site would earn a web surfer a chip, which they could redeem for cash and prizes.

It didn't take long before I met some interested investors who thought *Searchchips.com* was a great idea. I was able to raise $250,000 with the help of my friend, Glen Abbot, in three months to get the site off the ground in exchange for 20% of the business. I felt I had struck a pretty good deal for our seed capital; I really thought we were off to an amazing start. But guess what?

Starting a company is not easy!

Web Images

[   ] [Search & Win!]

Welcome!

SearchChips is a new search engine rewards website. Collect chips when you search, shop, invite friends, and bookmark. Then cash-in your chips for cool prizes. Everyone wins.
Learn More

▸ Get your FREE account now!

▸ Log in to your account!

Search & Win Instant Prizes

Search the web and win gift certificates and movie tickets instantly!
Learn more

Collect Chips & Get Rewards

Cash-in your chips for iPods, PSP's, digital cameras, and more.
Learn more

View Our Latest Winners!

Kristina, MD, Fandango Gift Certificate
Shavnda, NC, Fandango Gift Certificate
Jaavigness, IN, Amazon Gift Certificate
View more

About Blog Press Rules Help
©2006 SearchChips

In reality, I didn't have a clue what I was getting into. I did not know then what I know now, which is, building a successful startup takes tons of diligence, savvy, experience, smarts, luck and most importantly, a rock solid plan for an amazing product or service. *Your big idea is going nowhere unless all those factors fall into place.*

I felt I knew all of this going in.

I thought I had recruited a talented team and done everything I could to make sure we had all of our bases covered. But if there is one thing I have learned in my 15 years in the tech startup world, it's sometimes there's no better way to learn than by learning the hard way.

A Great Idea Is Worthless If It's Poorly Executed

When I started *SearchChips*, I felt it was important to make a significant investment in building a beautiful site that would reward users for their loyalty. I used one of my connections at *Ask Jeeves* to ink a deal to power the search engine.

Our site was off to the races.

For some reason, I wasn't surprised when *SearchChips.com* was a hit out of the gate. Sixty thousand users later and we'd given away thousands of iPods, iPads and Las Vegas vacations.

We were flying high and trending up.

Then, like that Icarus guy, we "flew too high on borrowed wings."

Like so many startups, we just couldn't sustain our success. What I had in energy and excitement for my business, I lacked in computer coding and technology experience. I wasn't a techie and was trying to run a tech company. How naively ambitious is that?

My biggest roadblock was I couldn't speak my people's language. I had to hire outside web developers to build my website; I had to trust people I didn't know and I didn't know anything about coding. I didn't understand how to host a website or setup a database server.

Looking back, I was way in over my head.

Never Invest In A Closed Source Website

My biggest mistake was hiring the wrong developer to build the site. When you screw up your first hire, you know you're doomed! I naïvely assumed any code our developer wrote for us was "open source," adaptable, and (most importantly) our property.

My assumptions were all wrong.

Turns out he owned the code.

After he developed the site, he began charging us a monthly fee to use it! Being a young guy, I couldn't grasp the concept. I just shelled out *thousands of dollars* to build a website that my partners and I do not own?

My mind was melting.

After some negotiations, it was clear the developer was never going to release the source code so just like that; my developer and I parted ways.

I wasn't beaten.

The good news was we still had $150,000 from the seed capital so I quickly hired another developer to build a *Searchchips.com* 2.0. We had to get the new site off the ground immediately because we still had 60,000 active users.

Now here is the punch line. *Searchchips.com* (2.0) wasn't as good as *Searchchips.com* (1.0)! No matter how hard I tried, I couldn't fix the bugs. The site was never the same again. My new developer tried but could not replicate the source code of my original developer. It was all too much for my non-tech mind to understand.

All I knew was my first startup was not going to work.

It was a tough pill to swallow, and hard lesson to learn about source code, but it is one that I still remember today: *Read the fine print before you sign any contract. Make sure your developer builds you an open source coded website that you own outright and can enhance any way you want.*

You're setting yourself up for failure if you fail to follow this one.

While all this drama was unfolding, to pour salt on my wound, I saw *Microsoft* was getting into the "search engine rewards business." Then I heard our primary competitor just got a windfall of cash by selling their site to *Publisher's Clearing House.*

Man, I thought, even if I raised capital to build a 3.0 site with a new developer, we were falling way behind our competitors in the marketplace.

So we gave back what was left of our seed capital, and shelved the idea.

It was a sobering realization to admit *Searchchips.com* was over – but it was.

So what did I do? Sometimes life is not fair. But you never give up.

Never. Ever. Give. In.

How Do You Say Inspiration? Yahoo!

Did it hurt to fail?

Heck yes, but I've never gotten hung up on regret. You can't. Entrepreneurs need thick skin. You have to keep moving forward, so I dusted myself off and said, "Ok, lesson learned. Thank you universe. I'm still young; no lives are ruined. It's just time for me to look for a job."

It just so happened that the first company I got an interview with was *Yahoo*. Wow, I loved that company! I remember during my interview, I talked about my experience with *AskJeeves*, and strategically omitted my *Searchchips* experience, which was a smart idea because I got the job.

I was really excited to say the least.

Yahoo was rolling out a whole new search advertising platform called Panama that I was going to be part of – and not to be a "dorky-tech fanboy" but *Yahoo* was one of my favorite companies of all time. I had admired them for as long as I can remember.

Yahoo didn't disappoint me. They are the most inspiring company I ever had the pleasure of working for, hands down!

Why?

Even though I was just an account executive, I was laying the foundation for who I wanted to be at *Yahoo*. I worked on the "Search Marketing" and "Display Advertising" side and managed over 20 million dollars a year in advertising investments. It was my job to know how to integrate advertising campaigns across the site.

I loved my time at *Yahoo* because I was thriving at a job that gave me "on the job" knowledge and experience in the web marketing tech world, which was very close to what I wanted to be doing as an entrepreneur.

I had a great time working for *Yahoo* for four years. They probably changed their website 50 times while I was there and went through five or six CEOs – so times were crazy but it was the people who made it a truly memorable experience.

To this day, some of the smartest people I know are *Yahoo* employees.

The Benefits Of Biding Your Time

I won't deny that during this time I also had a bitter taste in my mouth from the *Searchchips* implosion – so while I was doing a great job at *Yahoo*, I privately wanted to prove to the world that I could start another tech company.

I bided my time.

I didn't dive right back into founding another startup.

I stopped to regroup. I vowed to learn from my past mistakes.

I was going to be smart about my next venture so I put in the hours at *Yahoo*. I paid my dues, paid my bills and got savvier. I got smarter; I kept building my personal network.

Slowly but surely, I was plotting my next move.

I was learning how to be a savvy tech entrepreneur. And for that incubator experience, I can't thank the good people at *Yahoo* enough. You guys rock.

STEP ONE:

FIND YOUR PASSION, PURSUE WHAT YOU KNOW!

"The only way to do great work
is to love what you do."
— Steve Jobs

During my spare time at *Yahoo*, I began conceptualizing ideas for my next startup business. I remember I was home one day writing down all the things I love.

Why was I wasting my time doing that? Don't you know the happiest, most successful people in life do what they love? (That was something Steve Jobs really believed in!)

So I asked myself, "What do I really love in this world?"

It's a great question to ask yourself.

Why?

If you ask me, this is the first (and most important) step to building a profitable website! If nothing comes to mind, think back to when you were a kid. What got you excited? Do you have any hobbies that you don't have enough time to pursue? You may be able to turn your hobby into a profitable website. It could be a topic as broad as cooking, sports, travel, music – or as specific as parenting, playing bass guitar or hating your day job.

Whatever it is, try to uncover that passion within yourself then see if you can translate that into the world of commerce. Trust me, finding a business venture that you are sincerely passionate about will exponentially increase your chances of success.

I personally had a pretty long list of "things I love" – but at the very top of my list, I noticed other than technology, my greatest passion was music. I've always loved music. I was in a rock band for years so I thought, "You know what, that will make me happy." I want to do something that combines technology with the world of music.

So I drew a Venn diagram with the two intersecting circles. I started brainstorming what endeavors combined the two circles of technology and music.

I wrote down every combination I could think of.

Surround Yourself With Smart People

I spent a lot of time anguishing over this question but couldn't pinpoint a solution that spoke to my heart – so what did I do? When all else fails and you are out of ideas – *look to your personal network to come up with some ideas.* I brainstormed with a *Yahoo* colleague named Kevin Hein. He gave me some great ideas.

After our meeting, I decided to build an online forum for people to share their thoughts on music, artists, bands, singers and musicians. Kevin even gave me the idea for the name of the website: *AudioSugar.com*

I started to develop the concept based on one simple guideline: make sure this idea is something I would love to do 24/7. The next thing I did was write a business plan that included the unique features for the website.

Here are two:

1. *Audiosugar* would be a music community where users could create (then share) Top 10 lists like "Best bands of all time" or "Top 10 singers of all time".
2. *Audiosugar* would house a database of every artist, album and song. The site would be integrated with a recently launched product from Apple called iTunes, which would allow people to discover and download new music through this community.

It was a big idea but I was up for the challenge.

The Best Entrepreneurs Roll With The Punches

I knew from past experience, *Audiosugar* would not happen overnight. It would take a lot of time and capital to build right.

Meanwhile reality struck; the 2008 recession hit and it affected everyone, including me. *Yahoo's* business was going through a lot of changes; I sensed the turmoil within the company and decided to interview with another tech giant, *Amazon*.

Why would I leave a job I love?

My gut was telling me something was wrong at *Yahoo*, so I took a chance. I interviewed for a position with *Amazon's* new advertisement sales division. During my interview, I found out *Amazon* was building a new product called the *Kindle*, which intrigued me.

I thought if they offered me a job I would take it – and fortunately they did.

It was really hard to leave *Yahoo* but as fate would have it – a few days after I accepted the *Amazon* job – *Yahoo* laid off most of my division. It was a sad day at *Yahoo* for many of my colleagues, but more like a bittersweet day for me.

It was tough to say goodbye to all my friends, but the good news was I was going to a great new job and was even getting paid *Yahoo* severance for the first three months I worked at *Amazon*.

When I arrived for my first day of work in *Amazon's* New York offices, I was super excited to soak up all the knowledge I could. I had such a great experience with *Yahoo* I thought, "*Amazon* could only be better, right?"

Not exactly.

Once I got comfortable at *Amazon*, I realized it was a great company with a lot of great people – but working for them wasn't a perfect fit for me. I won't bore you with the details but let's just say the culture was very different from *Yahoo's*.

Although I learned some important business fundamentals while I was there, I did not stay at *Amazon* long. I decided if I wanted to be my own boss, it was time for me to get back out there and find my way in the world as an entrepreneur once again.

STEP TWO:

BUY A URL THAT GENERATES PASSIVE INCOME

"The moment you make passive income
part of your life, your life
will change."
— Robert Kiyosaki

You Need Money To Make Money

Knowing it would take some time (and money) before I was able to build *AudioSugar* properly, I wanted to earn some income to help me get through the transition from having an extremely high paying job at *Amazon* (with benefits) to being a self-employed tech CEO again.

The first thing I did was purge myself of anything I could sell. Any cash I could get my hands on, I stashed away. I didn't want to have to go back and work another corporate job ever again – so I was frugal as hell. By now, my wife also had our first child on the way – so I could no longer fly by the seat of my pants.

It was "do or die" time for me.

So many people give up on their dreams for a steady paying job in order to support a newcomer. I was determined not to fall into that trap.

After saving a good amount of money, I made a budget. I estimated I could only pay my bills for maybe three or four months on the money I had saved.

What would pay my bills after that?

Here is another lesson to file away: *Sometimes you don't have to invent the idea to profit from it.* What do I mean? There are a ton of internet "assets" already out there that already make money, many of which are for sale!

If you are looking to guarantee a flow of consistent, incoming revenue, my advice is to *consider buying an asset or company that is already a proven success.*

I'm not talking about a big time company; I'm talking about a small one that can generate a few thousand dollars a month to keep you going while you develop your own "big idea."

This is exactly what I did after I left *Amazon*. I knew the smart move would be if I could parlay the money I saved into an asset that can be a revenue generator. So I researched hundreds of websites that produced *"passive income,"* which is money that you don't have to actively work to earn.

I'm telling you this is a great way to fast track any internet venture without needing to raise VC money. This is not an original idea, you guys! We've all read *"Rich Dad, Poor Dad"* by Robert Kiyosaki, and if you haven't, you should.

I really took Kiyosaki's lessons to heart. You should too.

An Active Search For Passive Income

So there I was, inspired by Kiyosaski's amazing book and looking for passive income sources. I remember one day, I was searching for music on *Google* and came across an image of Jimi Hendrix that was the size of my desktop background. I liked the image so I clicked to download it, and immediately saw an ad right next to it for *StubHub* concert tickets.

The site was called *WallpaperPimper.com* and it was a place for people to download desktop wallpaper backgrounds. I researched their site and found they earned income from the ads (next to each image) and had more than two million images ranking on *Google*.

WallpaperPimper looked like a consistent passive money earner so I sent an email to the site's owner, who said the site earned around $2,000 per month in advertising. After some negotiating, I decided to spend my *entire life savings* (around $70,000) on purchasing the website. I estimated the site would pay for itself in three years if all went according to plan – then I would own this cash cow outright, forever.

This was another bold move. But I'm telling you, you have to take bold actions in order to succeed in this business!

So I told my family about my decision and naturally, they still thought I was nuts! They said I was taking too many risks and never should have left *Amazon* – and they had a point!

I knew I could lose everything on this one investment. I also knew there was a major risk to owning a site where users could upload copyrighted images, even though there was a DMCA copyright act (at the time), which protected these types of sites.

But I was undaunted. I was on a mission to find the cash flow to help me pursue *AudioSugar*, no matter what.

Little did I know, what was ahead of me.

Walking The Passive Income Tightrope

All I knew for certain was, it was time for me to experience a "trial by fire" learning experience like no other. I was counting on *WallpaperPimper.com* (my newly purchased profit arm) to provide a nice cushion of capital each month while I worked on turning *AudioSugar* into a reality.

I was still really young but I felt like I had a rock solid business plan for this one ... so much for "best laid plans."

WallpaperPimper ran smoothly for about a week!

The first issue we encountered was the obvious one: copyright infringement. I started to receive a bunch of "cease and desist" letters from large companies like *Red Bull* and *Toyota* who were threatening to sue me if I didn't take down copyrighted images that users had uploaded to the site. It took constant maintenance to keep the site clean but I stayed one step ahead of the lawyers on that one – one problem down!

But even with the copyrighted materials under control, I was still under a lot of pressure to make sure nothing else went wrong. I was walking a tightrope with no safety net. I had to make sure our server was always operating at lightning speed.

I was fully committed; I was going to "will this" baby to success.

Passion Projects Are Nothing Without Great Execution

I thought my plan was working to perfection. I thought I was on top of everything.

Then the "mother of all issues" hit us like a bolt of unexpected lightning. The disaster was no act of nature; it was totally man-made and it really hacked me off (no pun intended). What am I talking about?

WallpaperPimper was attacked by a mysterious Chinese cyber-hacker (who was posing as a Russian cyber-hacker). I'm not making this up!

Oh the intrigue. Except my hacker wasn't trying to steal government secrets … my hacker was looking to commit credit card fraud!

I saw what was happening and frantically hired a team of developers to "put out the fires" and secure the site. I felt really violated since my life savings was invested in this website – so, to quote the movie *The Godfather*, we "went to the mattresses."

I treated it like it was World War III.

My coders closed all "doors and windows" on the site but the hackers found their way back in through the "basement." Watching the whole thing was like watching a movie of my life turn into a really boring Jason Bourne movie. After investing way too much time and money into wiping the site clean, it was clear my team couldn't shake these insipid hackers completely.

The site was never the same after the cyber-attack.

I was living a web horror movie.

All I could do was watch the entire shit show sink into the ocean. I had to sell the website for a measly $2,000 – but guess what?

The investment still paid off!

In the two years I owned the site, *WallpaperPimper* earned nearly $3,000 a month (for a total of $72,000) so I "broke even" earlier than I estimated. I definitely got what I needed out of it. The passive income I earned was used to pay my bills and fund my path to becoming an entrepreneur. So it wasn't a total cluster of cyber-failure. It was painful but it worked.

A Passive Primer To Your Big Dream

Managing a passive income site had a learning curve, but it was well worth it to me. Is it crazy for me to think it would be for you too?

Don't be freaked out by the issues I encountered, they were totally natural (except for the Chinese cyber-hacker, which was a little out of the ordinary) – but this is the internet we're talking about here! Crazy stuff is going to happen. You just have to find ways around the roadblocks. All of you entrepreneurs reading this book should be able to grasp that fact.

Still need some convincing that owning a passive income website is for you? Don't just think about it as owning a digital "money-tree," though owning a passive income website is also an excellent crash course in business management.

Let's say you're interested in tech but are not a trained coder. The skills I acquired while managing a passive income site taught me a ton about website development and maintenance. I had to solve a lot of server and database management issues that I'd never seen before while maintaining, optimizing and growing a website (that literally meant the world to me.)

What better business technology training is there than that?

STEP THREE:

ALWAYS BE PIVOTING

"The only thing standing between you and
your goal is the bullshit story you
keep telling yourself as to why
you can't achieve it."
                                    — Jordan Belfort

Never Give Up On A Good Idea

Look at you "baby-stepping" your way to the promise land; I'm impressed. What? You're already tired? Don't get discouraged now that the road appears even longer (the longer we have walked on it) – just keep moving toward your final goal.

There are going to be a lot of people telling you that you can't do it and to give up. Tune them out.

Get in the habit of not making excuses.

Start thinking (and talking) about all the reasons why you "can do it."

Don't let circumstances dictate your future.

If you don't think you have the money, raise money from your friends and family. Apply for a line of credit with your bank, take on some debt; sell some of your property. If you don't think you have the time, find the time!

Moonlight after hours or wake up earlier and work a second job if you have to.

The goal is to delete the word "excuse" from your lexicon.

I'm telling you, if you can find a way to have a positive attitude at all times, the universe will meet you halfway. Put in the time and effort, and you're going to find all the answers to how to succeed through research, hard work, and trial and error.

Just by the fact that you are reading this book, I can tell you are a seeker, so keep stalking what you want in life like a fearless warrior. In a world full of online trolls, the only time you should accept "negative feedback" as the "truth" is when you are dead and buried. Why?

Think about it: death is the only circumstance you can't negotiate or pivot out of, right? Everything else is just an ongoing, evolving storyline. So don't let anyone drag you down. It doesn't matter how bad you screw up one of your startup businesses, if you are still breathing – guess what?

You live to fight another day ... and you can't ask for much more than that in this world.

Always Be Pivoting

It's a Cardinal Sin to give up on a good idea – don't do it! Write this down: *ABP*. What does ABP mean? It means Always Be Pivoting.

Don't you know that "pivoting" off a good idea to create an even better idea is the name of the game in the tech world? It's so true! With tech always improving – you have to operate under the presumption that there will always be a better way to do things (technologically speaking) – so never stop innovating. ABP!

Never accept that the "status quo" will remain the same very long.

That's what I did after I sold out of *WallpaperPimper*. After dealing with the cyber-hackers, I decided I didn't want to hang my hat on wallpaper sites, especially ones with a name like *WallpaperPimper*, which wasn't exactly something I could brag about to my old *Amazon* and *Yahoo* clients. But I still wanted to build off the good seed idea.

I thought, "How can I pivot off of this? What else can I do to make some passive income on the internet?"

Pivoting Into Premu Media

Luckily, around this time, I met up with a friend, Burt Breznick, who had experience working at *advertising.com,* as well as other advertising networks. Burt and I started talking about our careers.

After Burt listened to all my misadventures with *SearchChips.com* and *WallpaperPimper.com*, he said he was interested in becoming an entrepreneur too. It must be in Burt's DNA because I certainly didn't make it sound glamorous – but Burt clearly had the entrepreneur bug so we started talking about ways we could get into business together.

Burt and I did our homework and looked at a lot of possible deals but could not find a passive income site that appealed to both of us. I was about to throw in the towel – then I had a breakthrough.

I decided, forget wallpaper sites. Forget music sites (for now). I still wanted to buy a passive income site – but what if we never found one we liked? What if we switched gears entirely and created a "daily deal aggregator site," sort of similar to *Groupon.com?*

That kind of website (if executed well) would provide some nice passive income. Just look at *Groupon*, which at the time was growing faster than any company I had seen. I thought it was a great idea. Burt loved it too so we decided to get into "daily deal" market as fast as we could.

We built a site from scratch called *Premu.com* that was going to be an aggregator of all of the deals you could find on sites like *LivingSocial* and *Groupon.*

What differentiated *Premu* in the marketplace?

In theory, it was our integration with social media. No one was doing that at the time. We started to build an application around the daily deals and a social platform where users could share deals and even get credit when their friends bought into deals with them.

Sounds like an awesome idea, right? I thought so. Burt thought so. Our investors thought so. But our execution once again was not ideal.

What happened?

The development of *Premu.com* went way over budget and took far too long to build. Our speed to market was too slow and (in the end) our technology wasn't great due to our below average developers.

When *Premu.com* didn't become a big hit, I was disheartened (but not discouraged). I kept telling myself,

"Trial and error, trial and error." I knew we were getting closer to success with each incarnation.

Burt and I talked about our next move.

We didn't want to totally give up on the concept of *Premu.com* so we pivoted our idea again (into a completely different space this time, advertising.)

We created *PremuMedia*, an internet advertising agency that offered our skills and services to help advertisers.

Well, this pivot was a hit!

We recouped our investment on *Premu.com* in a couple months!

This pivot was a testament to our dedication and proof that "pivoting off of what we already knew" gave us a better chance of success than throwing it all away and starting again. This is great advice for all of you starting out.

Don't throw the baby out with the bathwater.

If you know you have a good idea, "Always Be Pivoting" off of it.

Pivoting Into The Present Day

I want to give Burt a lot of credit. He was a great business partner; he really pushed me to exceed our performance levels every step of the way. Burt was instrumental in helping turn *PremuMedia* into a profitable venture. The success of *PremuMedia* also got Burt totally infected with the "entrepreneurial bug" (that, no doubt, you are familiar with.)

Burt got a taste of success and said, "Let's keep going, let's pivot again!"

I said, "What do you have in mind?"

Burt challenged me. He asked if I would be interested in leveraging my experience at *AskJeeves* and *Yahoo* to create "something new" in the search engine world.

That is all he said. Something new?

I thought about it for a long time. I was intrigued but I could not come up with any great new ideas. Then, when I felt like "all was nearly lost," I finally had another "eureka" moment.

I came up with an idea for a website called *SearchMicrosite.com*, which I would later rebrand to *SearchMarketers.com* (after buying the domain name from a previous owner). *SearchMarketers* is my current internet marketing company.

As I mentioned, *Deloitte Fast 500* recently ranked us the 4th fastest growing company in the United States, which is pretty cool. Always Be Pivoting!

25 Steps To Internet Profits

Looking back on my career, I can say with all honesty I never would have been able to create any of my businesses if I had not leveraged all of the insights in this book to my advantage.

I want you to be successful too, so this book is my gift to you. I urge you to take these 25 steps to heart. If you do, I promise you'll have a better understanding of how you can start earning real money off the internet. It's a tricky balancing act (I know), but if you can combine a great idea with the right knowledge and "unbending intent" to get the job done, the internet can make money for you, every second of every day.

It doesn't matter if you're a web "newbie" or a seasoned professional looking for inspiration to build a bigger business online, the steps outlined this book can help you achieve your biggest internet dreams. Don't just take my word for it. The largest internet companies in the world are using these lessons to make money – so I hope you take good notes!

Even if you're not taking notes, I've got you covered.

I've found one problem with truly absorbing books (like mine) is being able to remember the resources listed – that is why I included a handy reference guide at the end of the book with all the links so you can revisit them as you work on your internet venture.

So what are you waiting for? Now that you know a little about me, let's do this thing (together). I guarantee if you work hard, stay focused and follow my lead – you can let the internet do the rest.

Now let's get to work.

STEP FOUR:

RESEARCH A DOMAIN NAME

"If opportunity doesn't knock,
build a door."
— Milton Berle

A Name Isn't Everything (But It's Huge)

I know "genius doesn't punch a clock" so if you haven't come up with your big idea yet – that's okay, these things take time. Since you and I only have a few hours, for narrative purposes, let's assume you're going to have your moment of inspiration very soon. In fact, *let's say you just had it right now*. OMG, you have an amazing idea for a new internet business. Congratulations!

I knew you'd always do it. I can't tell you if your idea is going to be great (only the market and people smarter than me can tell you that). But what I can say is, if you aren't sure about your idea – let it steep.

Ruminate on the possibilities.

Talk to trusted friends.

Do your research.

Are you still in love with it? Now ask yourself: can you see yourself raising money to build this idea of yours? If the answer to all of that is a resounding "yes" – awesome!

You may have struck gold with this one.

Have you thought about what you are going to call your "big idea?"

Names are kind of important. It doesn't matter if you're a human, a business, an app or a boat – being blessed with an amazing name is a huge plus so don't choose one lightly.

Here are some helpful tips when brainstorming yours business name:

1. **Be creative**. No one buys a product called "Meh" or "Blah," do they?

2. **Be confident**: No one is rushing out to buy a product called, "Poorly Made Crap," right?

3. **Be relevant**: Make sure your name evokes a product or service (somebody, somewhere) wants to buy!

Your goal should be to come up with a name that is fresh and clever while also being familiar and relevant to consumers. I'm no branding wizard so I don't have the "skins on the wall" to tell you how to come up with your company name (there are entire books written by experts on that).

But if you need some tips on how to pick out a domain name – I'm your guy.

Catchy, Clever & Relevant

The first step in picking out an awesome domain name is to choose one that is relevant to your business. Don't be too esoteric. Businesses with random names like "floozoo.com" or "kinzo.com" or "pongo.com" may be good for startup sites (with venture capital funds), but they are not very smart for building a grassroots fan base from the ground up.

Why not? They are hard to remember!

Let's say you love to play the bass guitar. You dig it so much you want to start a website all about it. What are you going to choose for your domain name?

I suggest rather than picking a "cute" name like *bassingguitarze.com* – try a more practical domain name like *playbassguitar.com*. Think about it: no one searches the web for "bassguitarze." So don't overthink this one. If you make your domain name something easy to remember, it will help your website make money faster. Why?

That's simple: because of *Search Engine Optimization (or SEO)*.

Want To Be Noticed? SEO Is Key

This is probably a good opportunity to explain how search engines work!

Search engines crawl the web looking for keywords that match the searcher's keyword query. Search engines love finding exact keyword matches in URLs (like "play bass guitar," for example).

They do not like misspelled keyword matches like "play bass guitarz."

Ideally, you want to include at least one commonly searched keyword in your business name; it would great if you could include more than one. If you can, your site will be in excellent position to climb the search engine results ladder – no matter what search engine a person uses.

What if you start a website that doesn't have a popular keyword in the domain name? I'm not going to tell you that you're doomed, but I can promise it will be a longer road to get your website to climb the SEO ranking to #1.

Give yourself a better chance by not getting too cute. Remember, the goal for your website is to become the #1 ranked search result on all search engines. If you can get the #1 ranking on *Google* – then you're doing great (because truth be told) the rest of the search engines out there don't matter nearly as much!

Domains + Keywords = SEO Heaven

Why are we discussing search engine queries so early in the book? Get used to it. SEO is the most important method of internet marketing out there. Why?

SEO gets your business in front of eyeballs on the internet!

Later in the book, I will give you some great SEO tips that will help boost your search rankings and drive traffic to your website (all without spending much money). Trust me, SEO is a great investment!

Brainstorm Keywords For Your Business

Back to the matter at hand: you really don't want to settle on a mediocre domain name so let's do some more research and see if we can add one (or two) "high volume keywords" into yours.

Here is a mental exercise: I want you to think about a few keywords that apply to your business somehow. Imagine you are *Googling* your big idea. What words would you use to search for (say) a website that features your big idea?

Write down a list of the top 20 keywords that come to mind.

If you need help brainstorming, I suggest you find out what keywords are popular around your big idea. How would you find out that information?

Simply use your gmail (or *Google* login) to access the *Google Keyword Planner*.

It's an amazing resource, why you ask? It takes you "behind the scenes" of search engine queries and shows you all the relevant keywords for any website on earth! How awesome it that? Not only that, you can also type in your own keywords and the *planner* will give you a list of related (searchable) keywords that are popular and relevant.

Want to know the best part?

The *Google keyword planner* will also tell you how many people searched for each keyword in the last 30 days, which will give you a great idea of which keyword(s) to target. Here is a hint: use keywords that are the most popular in your area of expertise!

Spend some time getting to know how it works. This website is going to become your most important tool while you do your research.

- Google Keyword Planner |
  https://adwords.google.com/KeywordPlanner

Remember, you have to build your domain name around a keyword that has high "volume," which means people are actually using it to search for information that relates to your big idea.

Choose one that's trending up.

Don't settle for the first one you find.

Why should you settle when you can "test drive" a bunch of them? Pitch them to your friends and see which keywords stick. Then see what words resonate with you. When you find a keyword that you like, make sure it has "spiked" in the last year, which means people are actively using it right now.

If it has spiked in the past year, your keyword is a potential keeper. You just need to find a way to build it into your domain name.

Adding Keywords To Your Domain Name

Now that you've settled on a few keywords that you feel would be perfect to include in your domain – your brainstorming duties are not over.

Now it's time to be really creative!

I want you to brainstorm 20 domain names that include your new keyword (or keywords). Say you are starting a "solar energy housing company" and you find out that people searching for "green homes" has recently spiked on Google.

Keywords like "buy" "green" "homes" are trending high so you want to include as many as you can in your domain name, right?

You could brainstorm domain names with popular keywords by coming up with names like: "Greenhomes.com," Buygreenhouses.com" or "Greenhomesforsale.com."

See what I mean? Let your imagination run wild. But don't get too cute.

Make Every Letter In Your Domain Name Count

You can even customize your ".com" extension if you want to really highlight that you're working with solar energy.

What do I mean?

Maybe you haven't heard, but there are an enormous amount of new extensions available that are industry-centric. You probably heard of extensions like ".org" or ".co" but how about extensions like ".DEALS"?

In this day and age, you may be able to purchase a domain name that literally mentions your specific business inside a custom URL extension. These extensions don't use the standard ".com" or ".org" – they end with things like ".INSURANCE" or ".SOLAR".

Do your research and find out if any custom extensions are right for you.

Back to my "solar housing" example – if this was your "big idea" you could conceivably register a custom domain name: "Buygreenhomes.solar" if you were to find out that "Buygreenhomes.com" was taken.

Pretty cool, right? The internet is amazing!

The goal is to make every letter of your domain name to be super relevant to searches for your business, even your extensions!

Google Insights For Search

After you have gone down the proverbial "rabbit hole" and researched the heck out of keywords trends, then you "got creative" and brainstormed 20 possible domain names that include your trending keyword(s). I suggest you check out Google Insights for Search next:

http://www.google.com/insights/search/.

Why? This website provides a list of the top searches related to your keyword. It's a really awesome tool; you can see how your keyword (or keywords) has been used in *Google* searches *for the past five years!*

You may discover a keyword you like, that you thought was trending, is actually not when you see the larger picture. Or you may uncover a totally new keyword (relating to your original) that you never thought would be a popular search word – but after looking at *Google Insights for Search*, you see it's actually trending higher than the original keyword you were interested in.

It doesn't matter where you find your keywords; the goal is to find the perfect domain name for your big idea *any way you can!*

Happy hunting!

If "At First You Don't Succeed..."

Don't get down on yourself!

Since the internet has been around for almost three decades now, the reality is a lot of big companies have already bought up most of the popular domain names – *so don't get too discouraged if you come up with a great one that is already taken.*

There are still plenty of available domain names out there for you. Just play around with the keywords until you find a domain name that feels right (and most importantly, is available.)

Don't spend months on this project.

Whatever domain name you choose – it's not going to change the world. I know I said they are "huge" in the beginning of Step Four (I was trying to motivate you!), but the truth is your *business model* is what will put your website over the top (or sink your ship) so don't despair if you find that all of your favorite domains are taken.

Just make the best decision you can.

Don't agonize over trying to find the perfect domain name.

Just do your homework and *select the best domain name available.*

Remember, the internet's all about who gets to the digital space first so we don't want to spent a lot of time "focus grouping" your domain name or someone may beat you to market.

Let's get this big idea of yours up and running already before someone else does!

STEP FIVE:

REGISTER YOUR DOMAIN NAME

"We're still in the first minutes of the first day of the internet revolution."
— Scott Cook

Good Domains Never Stay On The Market

Now that you have found your perfect domain name, don't get too excited just yet. I suggest you visit www.goDaddy.com and make sure that your domain name is even available first! Cross your fingers no one has taken it yet.

Some of you may be wondering, "Why did I choose *GoDaddy?*"

There are a lot of other domain registrar companies out there, but I think *GoDaddy* is the best for domains. Feel free to go with another one you feel comfortable with. But if you aren't sure – and you're like me (and not a techy), you may find that *GoDaddy* provides you with a host of easy to use tools for managing your website. I promise I'm not getting paid to promote them (I didn't get any of their Super Bowl ad money) but I really think they are the best.

Whatever domain provider you decide to choose – get on their website and find out if your domain name is available. If your name is available, what are you waiting for? Snap it up; don't wait! The good ones go fast!

You can register your domain name for roughly $10 per year while most domains (i.e. websites) themselves cost $39.99 a year to host.

If you are worried about paying for web hosting, you can get "free hosting" by using online tools from Blogger.com, Wordpress.com, or Tumblr.com.

You may have noticed these sites are pretty popular these days. Many of the largest websites around are built using these free hosting platforms (and I'm not just talking about blogs, I mean real websites).

So choose the one that feels right for you and never look back!

Customize Your Domain Name

Whatever website content management system you decided to use, after you are 100% sure it is the one you want to use – you need to go to the "advanced" section of their site and look for the "customize domain name" section in order to customize yours. There are a ton of customization options (no matter what provider you use).

What exactly does customization entail?

Let's say you are starting a blog – you could customize the domain URL they provide to you such as: "Joeslife.blogspot.com" and update it to joeslife.com.

If you are using *GoDaddy* like me, you have probably noticed there a number of other offers included with your account. I personally would not bother researching things like "consolidating domain names" (in order to get $2 off your domain names) unless you have a lot of free time on your hands. I suggest you stick to the basics for now until your website is running (and most importantly, profitable).

If You Can't Find a ".Com" Try ".Co"

If you are unable to find your domain name with a ".com" extension at the end, check to see if your domain name is available with a ".net" or ".co" extensions. That's right all you ".com" snobs. Soon ".com" sites will be "old news" so don't worry about being stigmatized for going with something other than the typical ".com" extension. You'll be a trendsetter!

There has been a lot of really good buzz lately around a whole new set of domain extensions. Why are they so popular?

First, domains with new extensions (like .deals, .solar and .reviews) are new and people get excited about new things. Second, they can cost less than ".com" ones, which is always a crowd-pleaser.

Another reason is you can get better keywords in your domain names by using one of these new extensions. I'm telling you, a lot of people who are starting new websites today are gravitating to the new extensions.

If you're having trouble with finding a ".com" extension, I strongly suggest you check the new extension domain names before you throw in the towel – trust me, you won't be sorry you did!

STEP SIX:

GET YOUR WEBSITE ONLINE FAST

"The Web as I envision it, we have not seen it
yet. The future is still so much
bigger than the past."
— Tim Berners-Lee

Get On The Horse Already

So you've bought and registered your domain name? That is great!

Let's say you already have a 1.0 version of your website developed that is really rudimentary. I know what you are asking – "Should I launch my 1.0 site or wait to launch until I have perfected it first?"

I know from experience a lot of people in your shoes might worry about populating the site with a lot of fresh content before launching it. I really would not worry about that.

If you ask me, you can "wrap yourself around the twist" on this one if you think about it too much. Sure, you want your site to be as awesome as it can be before it goes live – but no one is going to care if your site is not perfect at this nascent stage.

So don't be such a perfectionist and get the site up already!

I've seen far too many people let their big idea "die on the vine" without giving it a chance to thrive in the sunshine because they were too afraid to show their baby off to the outside world.

I'll say it again: *Fear is a poor advisor.*

As soon as you buy your domain, you should make an attempt to put it online as fast as possible even if it's just a "Coming Soon" page. Why?

Many search engines look at "domain history" (i.e. the age of your website) as a key factor when ranking websites. So the sooner you launch your site – the sooner search engines can find you and start counting you.

Again, I'm talking about SEO here.

You want search engines to recognize your site as a real live functioning web entity – and that will never happen if it is sitting in your garage collecting dust while you tinker with it incessantly.

See what I mean? It doesn't matter how much of a perfectionist you are, don't wait to get your baby on the open road of the digital superhighway.

I'm not saying rush a piece of junk to market! I realize there can be a lot of tricky steps when it comes to ordering your web hosting, configuring your files and developing your site (with HTML code) or even with using a software program like *DreamWeaver*. I totally get it. Some people see all those "technical barriers" and don't want to screw it up so they work on their site by themselves until it is perfect.

This sounds like a solid plan – *but it's not the way to go!*

Here is a little secret: Virtually every website on Earth launched before all the bugs were identified and removed! So don't feel like you have to iron out every one of yours before you go live. Get on the horse already and let your users work out the bugs for you!

Customize Your Settings

Here is one essential step that everyone must check off before your site can "go live" and that means editing the custom settings on your new website.

It doesn't matter what platform you decide to use, you will need to follow their instructions to change your DNS or "Cname record" at *GoDaddy*.

What the heck is a Cname record? It's simply the IP address that your domain points to, which ensures your website is "live" on the internet.

Here's how you can change (or edit) your site's Cname record using GoDaddy:

1. Log in to your *GoDaddy* account.
2. Next to *Domains*, click *Manage*.
3. Click the domain you want to use, then select the *DNS Zone File* tab.

4. Click the *www record*.
5. In the *Points To* field, type ghs.google.com.
6. Click *Save*, and then click *Save Changes*.

Your website is now "live" at your purchased domain name!

STEP SEVEN:

DESIGN YOUR BUSINESS LOGO

"Details are not the details.
They make the design."
— Charles Eames

A Great Logo Is Worth A Thousand Words

Creating a memorable logo for your business has never been as easy as it is *right now*. In the past, during the "Paleozoic Era" of the internet, designing your logo, brand or website could cost you as much as fifty thousand dollars. *Not today*. With all the young and hungry designers out there, you can find a talented designer (or a group of talented ones) for way less than you could even a few years ago.

And the best part is their work will be just as good as the high-priced designers from a few years ago. I'm not making this up!

All that said, it is very important that you follow a specific process if you want to get the best results for the most cost-efficient price. Remember your brand, logo and color scheme are the "it factors" that will make your website memorable and help differentiate your business in the crowded marketplace.

So don't take this step lightly, you want to make your work here really count. *It's that important.*

Those Who "Wing It" Pray For Success

When it comes to the design of your logo (or website for that matter) you can't just "wing it" and hope it magically will work out. *You need a plan.*

Some of you may know a graphic designer who is willing to help you design your logo for free. I don't want to tell you not to trust a friend but (from my experience) *if you want the job done professionally, you should hire a professional designer.*

If your friend is a professional, hire him or her to design your logo. You will be amazed how the quality of their work improves when you are paying them!

I know, I hear what you are saying. You are worried about the cost of hiring a professional, right? Well, don't start biting your fingernails or stress eating; I know you're on a budget. I got you covered!

Yes, there are thousands of talented design firms who will charge you a pretty penny to design your logo. We are not there yet so let's spend some time talking about where you can find the "best bang for your buck."

99designs: A Designer Collective

If you want my advice on where to get a great business logo, I'd steer you to a company called *99designs.com*. Why are they so great?

They aren't one of those typical high-priced design firms that employees a handful of elite designers – *99designs* gives you access to literally hundreds of designers in their network (from all over the globe) who want to *compete for the chance* to have your business. Sounds pretty cool, right?

99designs does not charge an "out of this world fee" – but that doesn't mean they provide this service for free. They charge (what I call) a "well worth it fee." I'm telling you, *99designs* really gives you great value for your dollar!

Their value proposition is two-fold: They do great work and give you lots of options, and as we all know, having a broad spectrum of choice is a huge factor to finding the "perfect anything." The more ice cream flavors you have to choose from, the better the odds you will find the perfect one, right? The same thing goes for logos. *The more logos you see, the more likely you will find one that suits your business.*

99designs will give you a broader assortment of logos (to choose from) than most of the high priced design firms ever would – which is awesome. I promise you will get the best logo possible when you have multiple designers creating multiple concepts.

I have a few horror stories where I paid a single design firm to come up with a logo who just "didn't get" what I wanted, but they had such a great reputation I trusted them. Well, guess what happened?

The high-priced design firm never "got" what I wanted and I ended up spending a lot of money and having to choose between a small group of logos that I didn't truly love. Don't make the same mistake I did! *Let multiple designers have a crack at your business through a company like 99designs!*

Competition Produces The Best Results

I'm not saying you *have to*, but if you *decide* to go with a company like *99designs*, once you've signed up for their service, you need to fill out a questionnaire then launch a *logo design contest.*

Once you have done that, designers in their network who want your account will throw their hat into the ring. Don't just wait for a designer to find your contest. I suggest you also spend some time on their website looking at their designers' portfolios. See which ones attract your eye then invite them to join your contest. *The more designers that join your contest, the better chances you have to come up with a great design.*

As soon as the contest is underway, there will be an *initial round* where you will select a handful of designers to move on to the *final round* where you will pick your winning designer.

No matter what stage your project is in, *99designs* makes it really easy to give your designer specific feedback so you can get your logo exactly how you envision it. *99designs* has a wonderful feature that can really help you pinpoint your feedback, which (if you ask me) sets them apart from any other design firms.

Want to know what it is?

99designs lets you click on any part of the your design and add a comment right on that spot. This feature lets you quickly focus on a specific design component that needs attention. If you have ever worked with creative people, you will think this feature is a lifesaver! Gone are the days of writing long emails or phone calls that can be misinterpreted. Now you can pinpoint your feedback so your directions are crystal clear!

Happy 99 designing!

Every Color Tells An Emotion

After you have designed your logo, now you need to decide on the look, feel, and color scheme for your brand. What if you are colorblind like 10% of everyone living in the United States? I've got you covered! Check out the *Color Emotion Guide* below to find out which colors will have the right effect on your brand's clientele. Yes, I know it's printed in black and white, but you get the idea.

Before I read this chart, I personally had no idea the color "purple" evoked feelings of "creativity and wisdom" or that the color "orange" gave off a "friendly, cheery and confident" vibe!

If you aren't sure which color to choose for your logo, *pick a color scheme that matches the lasting emotion that you would like your customers to come away feeling after interacting with your internet business.*

Choose wisely. Ask for feedback. Create focus groups. Don't just go by your own "taste." Why? *You're just one person.* It doesn't matter how great of a "tastemaker" you think you are, everyone has a different aesthetic so don't pick a logo that only you love. *Select a logo that appeals the broadest segment of your target market.*

That's how you will reach the biggest segment of your clientele!

Never Go To War Swinging A Paper Sword

What happens if you design a logo that doesn't stand out? I don't want to tell you that you're should pack up your ball and go home (amazingly enough, some businesses can actually thrive with a sub-par logo) but I will say that you are definitely not helping yourself.

Remember, perception is everything. If your logo looks like a "Bush League attempt at amateur hour," you will be going to war armed with nothing but a paper sword. "Meh" logos mean people will forget your business the second they leave your website – so don't waste a bunch of resources on making paper swords.

Put the time and energy into "crafting" the right logo that's sharp as a razor and solid as a rock.

Build Lasting Relationship With Good Designers

Another great thing about *99designs* is that if you love how your logo turned out, you can continue working with that designer on future projects "one-on-one" without having to create any future contests. How do I know this? I'm not just a spokesperson for *99designs*, I'm also a client! I promise, the people over at *99designs* aren't paying me anything to write this. I'm just a happy customer who is sharing my experience with you. Through *99designs*, I've been able to build a lot of wonderful business relationships with some of the most creative designers from all over the globe. They have been so inspiring to work with; I'm no dummy, I know when I have something good going; I'm going to keep using them! How's that for a testimonial?

STEP EIGHT:

DESIGN AN AMAZING WEBSITE

For a successful technology, reality must
take precedence over public relations.
For nature cannot be fooled."
– Richard P. Feynman

Let Your Logo Flow Into Your Site

Now that you have designed an amazing brand logo and color scheme for your internet business, I think you have a great basis point to begin designing your website.

If you skipped the brand logo step, I strongly urge you to go back and create your brand, logo and colors *before* you begin designing your website. I've found you can run into cohesion problems when you try to build your site before you create your logo (like your brand logo doesn't flow with website). *This is all on you, the project owner.*

You have to give your designer as much information as possible if you want them to build your dream site *so give them your logo and color scheme first!* That way your designer can use them as inspirations to build a site that is the perfect companion to your brand. Believe me, hiring a web designer to build a site from scratch with no frame of reference just doesn't work!

Your Website Is An Extension of You

No one is going to care about your internet business more than you will. This is your baby so take ownership of your website! Don't throw it over the fence and expect your designer to solve all your problems. That's not their job!

Remember, designers are not business owners so don't try to lasso them into any of your high-level decision-making. Think of them simply as "creative tools." They are pallet, the paint and the brush – you (and only you) are the artist! It's really important that you do all the heavy conceptualization of your site yourself. The most discouraging phrase a web designer can hear from you is, *"I don't know what I want but I know what I don't want."*

This kind of client uncertainty is a nightmare for web designers, why? When you have no clue what you want, your designer may as well be throwing darts at a dartboard when it comes to understanding what kind of website you want them to build.

And if you let your designer "freelance" too often, you won't get the site you're dreaming of so give them all the guidance you can or it will be nearly impossible for your designer to create an amazing website that fulfills your vision.

If you want to be a great "guide" for your designer, "Have a vision." Or at least have a strong opinion!

Imitation Is The Best Form Of Flattery

Make it as easy as possible for your designer to fulfill your vision by *providing clear cut examples of what you want your website to look like.* Look at some of your favorite websites in your industry and ask yourself:

1. What part of this website do I like aesthetically?

2. Does this website have a similar strategy to my website?

3. What "calls to action" do my favorite websites showcase? Are these the same "calls to action" that I will need on my website?

Provide Clear Examples Of What You Want

Once you have identified a handful of "example sites" – show them to your designer and tell them why you love them. Be specific! Provide clear and comprehensive feedback about what you like and don't like. Remember, unless the site is trademarked or copyrighted, "imitation is the sincerest form of flattery."

Armed with all this information, your designers will have a great starting point for building your website!

Ideally, your "example sites" will have something in common with yours. Both of your websites do not have to do the exact same thing but make sure they (at least) have a similar functionality. Want a few examples of what I mean? Let's say you are starting a "subscription site." Make sure your "example sites" are also subscription sites! If you are building an e-commerce site? Guess what? Find out which e-commerce sites are killing it in your market space – then share those!

I can't tell you how important this is to your designer.

Designers love seeing examples like these, why? You are giving them a blueprint for your site! This really starts you and your designer off on the right foot when it comes to finding a way to monetize your site (which is a fancy word for making money off of it) because you are patterning your site after websites that are already making money!

In addition to "example sites" – you can also share individual components that you like with your designer. They can come from any site on earth.

Use your best judgment when sharing components. Make sure every "add on" is essential. For example, if you are going to publish a lot of fresh content on your website, make sure you have a design component which allows for new content to be displayed.

The last thing you want to do is to have to go back and redesign a component because you forgot an essential element!

Communicate With Your Designer

Besides *taking ownership* and *providing lots of examples*, how you *communicate* is also a crucial factor when designing your website. I know how challenging it can be to work with a designer that you are not very familiar with; maybe you're not a natural communicator or maybe your designer is not all that verbal – but sometimes it can be tough to properly communicate your exact vision.

I can't tell you how to be a master communicator but I can say *frequency matters*. Do your best to keep the communication lines open between you and your designer. Over-communicate if you have to! Never go radio silent. The more consistent feedback you can provide, the more "locked in" your designer will be on your project (day-to-day) and the better your finished product will be!

Visualize Your Site In Vertical Interchangeable Compartments

Here is another tip for attacking a site build with a new designer. Try to visualize your website in "vertical interchangeable compartments."

What the heck does that mean? It means work with your designer to break up your web development project into manageable sections, compartments, components – it doesn't matter what you two call them just so long as you take them on one at a time and tweak each component until they are perfect.

Don't just tweak every interchangeable component; *tweak every vertical component too*. If you take this approach, the odds are good that some part of any design your designer creates can be used (in some way) to benefit your website. At least that is the prevailing theory!

Leverage Every Project For All It's Worth

Another helpful tip when working with designers is do your best to get the most out of each project. Getting your internet business off the ground is going to cost valuable resources (in the form of cold hard cash) so don't waste a single penny. *Squeeze every ounce of production out of every dollar you spend!*

One big "no-no" along these lines is never ask your designers to "remove" any component they have already built. *Only pay a web designer to "add" to your site design.* Why? Time is money. Don't pay them to remove a component they already built! You can always remove a component *yourself* later in html (or in development.) And if you aren't 100% sure a component should "stay or go," you can always save that code and put it back in later.

Trust me, these kinds of "best practices" will help you get the most mileage out of your design at the most cost efficient price.

STEP NINE:

DON'T WAIT TO POPULATE YOUR SITE

"Don't wait for opportunity.
Create it."
— Anonymous

Now The Fun Begins!

Today is the moment you have been waiting for. Did you get any sleep last night? Are you as excited as I am for you? Just think back to where you started; it wasn't too long ago when all you had was a crazy dream. But then you kept working until you turned your dream into a great idea for a business – which led to the creation of a brand logo and business website.

Congratulations! *Your dream's becoming a reality right before your eyes* (and all because you bought this book!) Just kidding, I would never take credit for all your great work – you have done all this yourself!

Now that you've been given the keys to your new ride, let's take your site for a test drive, what do you say? Don't be afraid to go for it. The longer you wait, the greater the chance your site will get lost in the "noise" of the internet and be forgotten like yesterday's meme. Take action NOW.

Getting Search Engines To Crawl Your Site

The first step to internet life can be taken right now if you have the guts to do it. All you have to do is go to the "Settings" section of your CMS (Content Management System) and fill in the "Main Title" and "Description" for your website. This will populate the "meta data" and gives all the search engines scouring the internet the blessing to begin crawling your site.

This is your first breath of life. You won't see your site listed in *Google* search results immediately; it's not that easy! You have to keep following the steps I am going to lay out for you until *Google* and the other search engines find you. But, at least, you can say, *now you exist*. You are on *Google's* radar and that is a great thing!

Get To Know Your CMS Tool

While you are fooling around with that, spend some time getting to know your Content Management System! There are a lot of "bells and whistles" available on the backend interface of your website that may be able to take your site to the next level. But how would you know if you don't understand how your CMS works? Answer: You won't!

It doesn't really matter which web hosting or Content Management System you choose (WordPress, Tumblr, Blogger, Godaddy, Squarespace, to name a few) you need to know your CMS tool like the back of your hand!

Once you have digested all the backend tools at your fingertips, you can begin teaching yourself how to customize your website. I know what you're asking, "Wait a minute? I thought that's what I hired my developer to do?!" Well, yes and no.

There are always new "add ons" coming out that you can install yourself. They call these features "widgets" ("add ons" or "plug ins") and they are really simple to add to your site. All it (usually) takes is one click of a button. It can't get any easier than that, right?

This step may sound "technical" for a layman like you but it's not rocket science and frankly you need to learn to do small customizations yourself, why? *Customization is king in our specialized world.* You won't soar above your competition with a cookie-cutter website so you need to take it upon yourself to do all you can to make your site as cutting edge and user-friendly as possible. It's up to you!

Developing Killer Site Content

One of the most important secrets to creating "web profits" is your ability to develop fresh content. It doesn't matter how kick ass your website looks – content rules the internet – so think about what kind of information you want to present to the world. Your content can include *pictures, video, audio files,* or *text.*

As for what kind of content to load on your awesome new site ... *it's completely up to you.* Stake your claim on the internet any way you see fit but remember, the *Google Gods* will be watching.

Ok, I admit it. There are no actual *Google Overlords!* But there are *Google Bots* that are super important to your SEO. They want to see that someone is living in your house (i.e. your website). *Empty houses are overlooked and ignored!* When the *Google Bots* sees you have fresh content on your site, they say, "Look, someone is home after all," and will start to recognize your site as a legitimate entity.

And we all want to be "legit," don't we? Who doesn't?

Now, if you are not sure what content to load, create a "Coming Soon" page (for now) that tells people your content is forthcoming. This may sound like a pointless symbolic gesture but it's really not. Why? In the eyes of the *Google Bots* – your Coming Soon page is fresh content so it helps you become recognized as a legit site.

Don't wait to launch your site because your content is not perfect. Here is a little secret: it's never going to be perfect! To quote the *Nike Overlords,* "Just do it!" So have fun, be creative and experiment until your content has your unique stamp on it!

Put Your Unique Stamp On The Internet

I know what some of you are saying, "Geez, I'm not that unique. Maybe my idea is not as good as I thought?" Don't worry. You don't have to be "Andy Kaufmann unique" with your content creation to stand out in the crowd. All you have to do is be different enough to find an audience. Here is a good example of what I mean.

I have a friend who built a great website. He has a great sense of humor and is always telling jokes so a few years ago, he decided to "follow his passion" and create a blog in his spare time where he could write funny blog posts that showcase his unique brand of humor.

So he set up a free blog at Blogger and began to post original content in the form of funny articles (with embedded video content). He kept it up for several years. My friend (who shall remain nameless) isn't the next Dave Chappelle or Robin Williams, he just likes to share funny stuff he finds on *YouTube* and around the web. I know this doesn't sound like some huge revenue generating idea for a website, but guess what? The traffic on his blog kept growing, which was a testament to his comedy taste and his commitment to improving his site's SEO.

At one point, his blog got so popular, his sites showed up second on a Google search for his blog's specific keywords. That's nothing to sneeze at considering that particular keyword search returned *308 million websites in addition to my friend's.*

How did his site rise to the #2 ranking? It would have never happened if he didn't have a passion for comedy. He may have created a blog and added a few posts then decided not to stick with it but he used his passion for comedy to drive him to keep going. It's also a testament to his SEO skills and great eye for sharing comedic content.

You would think with all those hits, his blog would eventually become quite profitable. Well it would have if I were in charge of it. But I guess my friend wasn't as committed to the site as I thought he was. After a while, he got busy with his "real job" so he stopped updating it and let his domain registration run out.

Now his site is permanently "dry docked" in website purgatory.

What the heck happened?

His passion could only take him so far. His story goes to show that even if you create an awesome website with a big grassroots fan base, you can still fail if you aren't monetizing your site traffic. He did a great job of coming up with a really popular website but, in the end, he never figured out how to make enough money off it to make it more than a hobby.

What a shame because I loved his site!

Let's my friend's story serve as a cautionary tale; I'm going to show you how to maximize the profitability of your website so your amazing "big idea" never gets dragged down by a lack of funding.

STEP TEN:

SET UP YOUR SITE ON WORDPRESS

"Content makes poor men rich.
Discontent makes rich men poor."
— Benjamin Franklin

The Best CMS Tool By Far Is...

Now that we have discussed integrating your website with a Content Management System, which one should you choose? A lot of them are good but if you ask me, *WordPress* brings more options to the table. Believe me, you would be surprised to learn how many big corporate websites are built on *WordPress*. If you are going to publish a lot of content to your site, I suggest you go with them too!

If you are "starting from scratch" with your web design and want to get your content online quickly, one of *WordPress' Site Templates* could be a good option for you.

But if you want your website to really stand out in a crowd, I would avoid templates because a lot of sites already use them. Instead, I would have a custom logo and site created by a design firm (like *99designs*). Then you can integrate your custom site into *WordPress*.

I personally like to combine the custom web design of *99designs* with the easy-to-use CMS tool *WordPress*. If you take this route, I think you'll be on your way to a building a killer site that will blow your competition away. Not only will your site have the custom (interchangeable) design components, you will also have the ability to manage your site as you see fit.

And who doesn't want to be the *master of their own domain?*

More Awesome WordPress Features

If you're not exactly the "hands on" type of website owner, that's okay. A lot of people need help with their content management so *WordPress* lets you add authors, managers, admins, and users to the backend of your website.

WordPress also has an impressive array of "bells and whistles" (they call plug-ins), which are outside applications built by third party developers from all over the world. These are really great!

I urge you to spend some time exploring all that they have to offer. You won't be disappointed! Each plugin has its own description and reviews so you can find the one that best suits your needs. If you find a plug-in that would be a great addition to your site, you can add it with the click of a button. *It's that easy.*

But don't go crazy. You have to be discerning! It is crucial that you pick the right plug-ins for your site. You can't add every plugin that's available or your site would be an overloaded mess – so learn to *prioritize*. Think logically.

Site Security Is Priority #1

For example, you don't want to add a "Meme Maker plug-in" to your site before you've added the proper security plugin. Focus on your site security first!

If you have any forms on your site, I strongly urge you to protect yourself against spam with a plugin called *captcha code*. I had to learn this one the hard way with one of my passive income sites. When I launched that site (a few years ago), I let anyone post comments; I didn't even moderate them.

Big mistake! I noticed after a few months, my server was slower than normal. What happened?

The culprit was a hacker who was auto-posting hundreds of comments to my site! It wasn't nearly as bad as when my *WallpaperPimper* site was hacked, but it did make me wonder, "Am I the only one getting hacked?" I quickly found out that hackers come with the territory. If your website grows big enough, you will attract them so plan for it by setting up a strong security infrastructure that limits attacks.

Don't end up learning like I did; the "hard way" is never fun!

My Favorite WordPress Plugins

Can you believe that "way back in the day" all of the code for plugins had to be built manually? You have it easy these days! Now you don't have to understand html to take advantage of a wide array of plug-ins that will set your website apart from your competition.

Before you install any plugin – make sure you are always working with the most current version of *WordPress*, falling behind on an update may cause some plugins to not work. I know every single one of you are not going to use WordPress, but if you have gotten this far, you have to be curious, so here are a few of my favorite *WordPress* plugins for you to consider:

1. **All in One or Yoast SEO Pack Plug In**
   Great for SEO! Instead of learning to code and edit "meta data," which is the text search engines show to describe your web pages, you can easily control every "meta word" and help improve your site's *Google* rankings with this plugin

2. **Disqus Comment System Plug In**
   Encourages engagements, comments and replies in your talkback section.

3. **Really Simple Captcha or Akismet**
   Protects your site against spam comments and I'm sure you've seen them!

4. **Social Media Plugins (*Facebook, Pinterest, Youtube*)**
   Makes social media integration a breeze!

5. **Google XML Sitemaps**
   Puts your website pages into sitemap files, which helps *Google* find them easier!

6. **UpdraftPlus WordPress Backup Plugin**
   It's always good to have a backup of your work for a rainy day! This plugin does the trick.

7. **MailChimp for WordPress**
   Syncs your website with a *Mailchimp* account to collect subscribers for email newsletters.

8. **AddToAny Social Media Buttons**
   Add great social media sharing options into your site with this plugin.

STEP ELEVEN:

SET UP YOUR SITE WITH GOOGLE ANALYTICS

"Real knowledge is to know the
extent of one's ignorance."
— *Confucius*

If you have gotten this far in the book and you're still not comfortable playing the part of "savvy tech entrepreneur," don't assume that your internet business is going to fail just because you are not an "expert" web developer. Here is a little secret *the tech intelligentsia* will never tell you: *we are all faking it in some way.*

As much as techies like to brag they caught every hacker reference in the latest episode of *Mr. Robot* – trust me, they are not as smart as they seem! The tech industry is growing so fast and furious very few people can keep up with all the changes. Once you think you're an expert in something, a new advancement will come along that will turn all that you "thought you knew" into outdated information. So take comfort in the fact that full mastery of this subject is extremely rare. *Don't stress out about it.*

The next time you feel any doubt, work on identifying exactly "what you don't know" that is worrying you. Then find someone who has the expertise in this "problem area" and let them help you "patch that hole" in your game. Repeat after me: *You don't need to be an expert techie, coder or web developer to make money on the internet. All you need is a great idea for your business and a clear vision for how to achieve it.*

If you don't know what the heck a *Cascading Style Sheet* is – so what?

Hire people who do!

The key is not to let your insecurities prevent you from *making something happen.* I kept plowing ahead and it worked for me, and I'm definitely not an "outlier" in the industry, far from it! *I think I just wanted it more.*

I've personally met dozens of internet CEOs and entrepreneurs who know nothing about computers but still run very successful websites. What they lack in technical expertise, they make up in overall business smarts. In many cases, their lack of technical knowledge actually helps them focus on the higher level "mission critical" factors that go into running a successful business, like working with their VC/PE stakeholders or managing their P&L (Profits & Losses), which (relatively speaking) are much more important than any piece of code or technical know-how!

Patching Holes In Your Skill Set

I don't know what size of ego you are packing but if you are serious about improving your technology skills, I have always found it extremely useful to hire people who are much smarter than me. I am definitely not one of those insecure bosses who must be "right" about everything in order to feel good about myself. Maybe I'm in the minority here, but I actually feel comfortable saying, "I don't know, what do you think?" to my employees. Why? Because it's the truth and I've found people like to work for bosses who "tell it like it is." I feel like my collaborative attitude has gone a long way toward helping me "patch the holes in my game" and learn important information on the fly.

I'm not saying you have to follow my lead here, but when you realize you don't have the skills to complete one of the steps in this book (and you probably will), don't let fear of failure eat away at your confidence. Instead, I want you to identify what you don't know, then seek out an expert who will "fill your knowledge void" – and keep on trucking to the promise land.

Don't ever let "what you don't know" stand in the way of achieving your dreams!

At Least Learn the Basics!

Remember, the *SearchChips* story I told you about the developer who claimed the code he built for my company was "his" property? Accepting that excuse was a total rookie mistake on my part. Why did I make it? One big reason was I had not learned the fundamentals of web development yet. I didn't know then what I know now, which is: *You can get away with not being a tech expert but you can't get away with being a tech moron!*

You don't have to "learn it all" but do try to put some of this expert information you are getting from your "resident tech wizard" into your personal hard drive. At the very minimum, you should learn the basics of how to run your own website. "What is the point," you ask? *It's empowering! It's your business! It matters!* And once you have that basic understanding of how your site works, I guarantee you will never be at the mercy of a developer who tries to hold his knowledge over you. I'm not saying getting duped by web developers is a big problem in the industry, but the more you learn, the less chance that people will try to take advantage of you.

Remember: knowledge is half the power!

Measuring Goals On The Internet

I remember when I created my first internet advertising campaign. I ran it with no understanding of what the word *analytics* even meant! My campaign drove a lot of consumers to my website but I still lost tons of money, and the worst part was I didn't know exactly why.

See the recurring theme here? *I didn't have the knowledge I needed to succeed.*

Boy, did I learn this lesson the hard way! Have you ever heard the famous quote from John Wanamaker? *"Fifty percent of my advertising is wasted, I just don't know which half?"* That was exactly how I felt! Even an internet neophyte like me knew that "not knowing" was a very 20th century problem to have. I didn't make that mistake again and neither should you.

If you are running an internet startup today, there is no gray area when it comes to your site metrics because *everything on the internet is quantifiable.* Reach out and grab the data already, there is no excuse. You can track everything: all actions, all visits, all clicks and all video plays (to name a few). If you are the CEO of an internet marketing firm today and you drop the old "I don't know why half of our advertising isn't working," then guess what? You aren't a very good internet marketer!

Now, whenever an advertiser asks me to help with an advertising campaign, my first question is *"What is the goal (conversion, or objective) of your marketing campaign?"* If you ever work with a client who does not have an answer to that question, I recommend you not invest another minute with them until they figure out their goals. What if you are that client?

Well ... I would tell you the same thing I always tell my clients, "Once you have solid goal(s) in mind, then I can help you set up a 'tracking mechanism' that will use your goal(s) as a basis to quantify your efforts and measure your success rate."

What is the tracking mechanism of which I speak? That's easy.

The Power of Google Analytics

Before you read another page in this book, you have to have something called *Google Analytics* setup on your website. One amazing thing about using *Google* (and there are plenty of them) is they provide you with the best analytics and tracking tools for *no cost*. *Google Analytics* is super easy to setup. All you have to do is *copy and paste a snippet of computer code into every page of your website's code*. It's that simple.

After you've done that, *Google Analytics* will start tracking everything from your website's unique users, to page views, user location, time users spend on your site, and much more. Give it a shot. This is not a request; *it's an order!*

If you want to be a big fabulous internet hit, you have to know your audience. There is no reason you should skip this step my faithful reader. None. Nada. Zilch. So don't. You can thank me later! I don't want you to end up like all the people I met over the years who had great ideas for internet businesses but didn't "go for it" because they weren't techies. *Well, those people were flat out wrong.* My advice to you is "Just do it baby." If you have an unbreakable belief in your big idea, don't wait around for "paralysis by analysis" to take over. Take a leap of faith that you can do this – then keep going! Clearly see your technical limitations, but use it as motivation to get better by learning more about tech and "patching the holes in your game."

If you ask me, that is a winning recipe that *works every time.*

STEP TWELVE:

CLICK, LEAD, SALE, & CALL ANALYTICS TRACKING

"If you torture data long enough
it will confess to anything."
— Ronald Coase

Tracking Your Leads And Sales

Now I hope you understand how *vital* analytics are to the success of any website. Without accurate metrics measuring the right data, you won't be able to quantify your business goals in any logical way.

So let's just assume you're a "smart cookie" who is taking my advice and setting up *Google Analytics* on your site (I really hope you are right now). After inserting the *Google Analytics* code on to *all of your web pages*, *Google* is now watching all of the activity on your site. As we know, some website pages are more important than others so you need to specify exactly what pages (and what data) is most important to you. Once you've done that, *Google Analytics* will collect it for you.

What pages on your site are most important? It really depends on the business you are running. There are a zillion different metrics you can collect but for today's discussion, let's say you are trying to drive leads to your "life coaching" business, ok?

After a user submits a lead through your website, they should be taken to a "thank you" page that will capture all of your lead data. If you are in a business where lead tracking is a big deal, I highly suggest you set one of these pages up! After you have created your "thank you" page, you can enter it into *Google Analytics* as your specified "lead conversion goal" and *Google* will start tracking how many leads you are getting in real time on your website.

Similarly, if you are running an E-Commerce website, you could also create a "thank you" page that site users will be directed to after they order a product. If you ask *Google Analytics* to monitor this "thank you" page, you will be able to easily track your website sales.

Deeper integrations of *Google Analytics* can even reveal data like "revenue earned from each sale" but we won't delve into that right now. Just know that you can easily track any data that comes and goes on your website through *Google Analytics*.

Tracking Call Analytics

When it comes to metrics, one question I hear a lot is, "How do I track offline activities like phone calls back to the customer's website activity?" This is a great question. We may be living in the digital age, but a lot of companies are still built on driving customer phone calls to their business. So when people ask me, "Can this be done?" I say, "You bet!"

It is possible to track your phone calls in *Google Analytics* but if you ask me, it's much easier if you work with a "call analytics company" that will record (and track) every call to your business in real time. If driving phone calls is important to your business, now is the time to set up "call tracking" on your website, one way or the other!

My own personal favorite company for tracking call analytics is called *Invoca*. They allow you to setup (and place) local, long distance or toll free numbers on your site. I've used them for years and they make it very simple to track your phone calls. Plus, their interface is second to none.

The bottom line is you can track any data you can possible conceive on your website; sometimes *Google Analytics* can "do it all" but if you are in a business that needs custom data, you may need to outsource this task to a company like *Invoca* who specializes in granular data collection that you can't get any other place.

Good luck and happy data crunching!

STEP THIRTEEN:

PUBLISH ORIGINAL CONTENT TO YOUR SITE

"Content is king."
– *Bill Gates*

Did you know Bill Gates was the first person to coin the phrase, "Content is king?" Can you believe Bill said that back in 1996 before the internet was even a big deal? That was one prophetic statement. Two decades later, and "original content" remains one of the most vital elements of any successful, moneymaking website. Have you ever heard of a cool (profitable) website that had terrible content? *Neither have I.*

So now that you've gotten your website up and running, it's time for you to create some awesome content that will appeal to your fan base. In case you've been cryogenically frozen the past 20 years, "original web content" can be anything that people might consume on their smartphones while they wait in line at Trader Joe's.

Google Is Always Watching

I can't tell you what *kind* of content you should create, but I can tell you what *types* of content will get the "most bang for your SEO buck." And you should know by now that ranking high on Google is just as important as getting a million hits.

When brainstorming ideas, try to think like our *Google* overlords and focus on creating content that catches the eye of the *Google* bots, who are constantly scouring the web, looking for new content to link to. The best way to attract *Google's* attention is to create content they recognize. If you're using *Wordpress* (or any CMS tool) make sure to categorize all of your content into clear categories and store them like they were books in the appropriate files in your web library. If you have a *clean house,* it will make it easier for your users to navigate and for *Google* to crawl your site.

So what type of content is right for your website?

If you aren't sure, tap into the Zeitgeist. Look around. What do people spend their time looking at on the web? Do research and pattern your content after stuff you know that people are interested in. Don't aspire to be the most original URL in existence, aim to be the *most useful* in your area of interest. Why? If you create content that people *need*, rather than just *want*, your audience won't be able to live without you, which bodes extremely well for your website's future.

I know what you are saying, "But my site is a business site, not an entertainment portal." It doesn't matter what business you're starting, you'll need fresh content consistently posted on your site to stay relevant in the eyes of *Google*. Sites that only eek out a little fresh content (every so often) will be overlooked by the Google bots.

What if your business does not create fresh content naturally? Guess what? You need to manufacture it! Your fresh content can be anything from creating a business blog with *content marketing* stories that reinforce your brand – to something as simple as posting a bunch of funny videos or cat memes to your site. Maybe your site features photos you took, or songs you wrote, or pieces of digital art you created. It doesn't matter what type of content you post, as long as it's a natural extension of your site's reason for being.

A blog story about making the best Super Bowl guacamole would fit nicely on a home-delivery produce site, but not so much on a site that sells Russian andirons in the Czech Republic..

See what I mean?

Craft A Personal Narrative

A lot of company sites these days have blogs where the CEOs of some very respected businesses are posting fresh content daily. I think that is an amazing idea. If you are the CEO of your startup – but you don't want to put yourself in the spotlight, suck it up and do it for your business. Who else is going to be the face of your company, if not you?

Let's say you just built a site for your extreme vacation business. What will make your business stand out from your competition? *You will.* No one on earth is "just like you" so why not make yourself the face of your business? What are your interests? Do you like motorcycles, camping and making your own beef jerky? Right on, *Steve McQueen Grizzly Adams*, you have your blog topics right there!

You could write a blog post about whether your *Indian* motorcycle can get replacement parts while road-tripping through Europe, or you could shoot a video on how to make your own buffalo jerky, or tape a podcast that offers tips on how to set up your tent at 13,000 feet. See what I'm doing here? All of these content ideas are both informative and entertaining – and they relate to your business.

It doesn't matter what business you are creating – try to create a unique (yet useful) personal angle when crafting your content if you want to stand out in the crowd.

Repurposed Content Makes The Web Go Round

If you are worried about being completely original, *relax.* Today it is perfectly acceptable to create "repurposed" content that is sort of original and takes way less time to create. You probably read "repurposed" stories all the time on aggregator sites like *The Huffington Post* and *The Drudge Report.*

So if you are having writer's block, stop banging your head against the wall and go find an interesting story on the web that relates to your business – then "write a story about that story" and link to it.

Suddenly, you have fresh content you can post that did not take a lot of effort to create. Let "*Google* alerts" to do the research for you. *Google* will email you the latest articles about any keyword. It literally takes five seconds to set it up.

Say you are starting a fashion business. Why not setup a *Google* alert for the keyword "fashion?" If you do, every fashion-related article posted to the web that day will be sent to your email. I'm telling you, you have to stay on top of what is happening in your field of interest if you want your content to sing.

Trust me, there is no better way to ruin a website than by posting stale information that no one wants to read anymore. So stay current!

Commenting Feature

Everyone who owns a website wants theirs to be the "stickiest of the sticky" which means when a user stumbles upon their site, they can't take their eyes off it, why? Because it has so much new relevant content – you can't help but keep coming back for more. If you can get people spend more than a few seconds on your site, it will raise your search rankings and drive more traffic your way.

But how do you plan for stickiness, exactly?

One way is to post great fresh content! But another is to add a "commenting" feature to your site. If you are using, Wordpress, you can easily add it with a few clicks; it's a great way to allow your readers to engage with each other, which in turn will make your site stickier.

Do you want to know what company has maxed out the stickiness of its commenting feature?" Facebook. Their commenting tool is the gold standard today. Everyone uses it and it keeps people coming back to their site. If you set up your site using Wordpress, here is some good news. Your site can be fully integrated with Facebook.

All you have to do is set up the feature on Wordpress – and it will post any of your users' comments directly to your business's Facebook page, which will help drive more Facebook users over to engage in your content.

It's a win/win, so do it already!

Print Is Not Dead, Just Ask Google

I know you can probably outsource a lot of the tasks in this book to professionals you meet online, but for the love of humanity, don't outsource your content writing to a non-English speaking writer. I remember the late, great Harold "Egon" Ramis once famously said, "Print it dead" in the movie *Ghostbusters*. Sure, Egon was a smart dude who collected spores, molds and fungus, but he meant the "chopped down tree" kind of print, not the "printed word" kind, which has made a seamless transition to the 21st century, despite all the erroneous reports of it's demise. It's true, few people have the time to read phone book-sized tombs like David Foster Wallace's *Infinite Jest* or Proust's *Remembrance of Things Past* anymore – but billions of people still read smaller pieces of written stuff on their phones, all the time.

So don't kid yourself, all you "visual artists" who can't read or write; print is still one of the most popular forms of communication on the web. *Sites with unique, relevant, and authoritative text copy will naturally rank higher in the Google search rankings.*

If you want to create original written content but you aren't a strong writer, hire a professional writer. Don't skimp on this step; poor grammar will turn off your audience. You can find a good writer on freelance websites like *Upwork* who are reasonably priced and will save you a lot of time.

I learned the hard way on this one. A few years ago, I outsourced my content writing to freelancers I met on the web. Little did I know, but I hired people that did not know how to write (or speak) fluent English. Inevitably, my site, which had a lot of written content on it, ended up being stolen from other sites, and had a ton of misspellings. I'm not sure how you could copy someone's work and somehow *still misspell the words*, but it happened! Needless to say, that site quickly fell from the Google rankings. If you ever run into this problem, you can quickly find out if a writer you hired is using another person's copyrighted content on a site called copyscape.com.

A Picture Tells a Thousand Words

We are a visual species, always have been. We love to watch. We enjoy looking at pretty pictures so your site better have some that convey the right emotion(s) and keeps your users reading whatever written content you have created. It is very easy to upload photos you took (from your computer to your *Wordpress*-powered site) – but what if you need professional pictures that you can't do yourself?

I suggest you Google "public domain images" or pay a few bucks and get some nice stock photography images to go with your written posts. Just be sure to avoid breaking any copyright laws.

Remember my *WallpaperPimper* story? As the former owner of a "pimp your wallpaper" site, I know a few things about images! Can you believe most websites don't worry about copyright laws, at all? It's crazy but true. Most website owners simply steal pictures from other websites and use them for themselves.

Few get caught, but when you reach over a one million users on your website, you may get a "cease and desist" copyright infringement letter like the one I received from *Toyota* and *Red Bull* for having their logos on my site.

I promise; I didn't post those images. The images were uploaded by site users and governed by the DMCA copyright act, but that didn't mean it wasn't scary to receive those letters and have my website suddenly up against a monster like Toyota. They could have eaten me for breakfast. So keep it legal when it comes to posting images and your conscience will be clear, no matter how many millions of people flock to your site.

Video Content Never Goes Out of Style

Who doesn't like a funny, touching or informative video? Answer: nobody. Video is the ultimate medium that goes well on any site. If you are interested in posting your own video content, it might be a good idea to (first) create your own *Youtube* or *Vimeo* channel. If you post your videos on one of those sites, you can use the embedded link (or plugin) to easily post the videos to your site.

Don't try to be a professional videographer; know your limitations. With so many video-editing programs (like *iMovie* or *FinalCut Pro*), a lot of Junior Scorseses can get "delusions of grandeur" and get out of control with their videos, which inevitably results in hours wasted trying to edit together the perfect video. Don't try to win an Oscar. Some of the best videos are ones that are filmed with an iPhone. If you feel comfortable editing and "have a vision" for a video that will help drive traffic to your site, then by all means, go for it. But keep it simple. No CGI explosions, please.

Now if you're looking to create a high-end video like the one by Michael Dubin that put *DollarShaveClub* on the map, you definitely want to outsource that to a production company if you want it done right. However you do it, adding fresh video content will help your site tremendously because it extends the "engagement time" a user has on your site. And the longer they stick around, the better for you and your *Google* search rankings.

STEP FOURTEEN:

GET INTO THE GAME WITH SOCIAL MEDIA

"Good (social media) content always has an
objective; it's created with intent. It
therefore carries triggers
to action."
– Ann Handley

Promote Your New Site On Social Media

It doesn't matter if you started an online gaming company or you're making your own Kombucha SCOBY and selling it online, your website must generate a continuous stream of compelling new content if you want it to attract attention. Not only that, but you need to promote all of your new content on social media. If you don't have social media pages set up for your new internet business on platforms like Facebook, Twitter, LinkedIn, Google+, Instagram, Pinterst or Snapchat – get with the 21st century and create them already!

If you're saying, "But Joe, I don't have time for social media," what if I told you there are several ways to automate the posting process? That would save so much time, right? Here are two awesome ways to incorporate social media into your internet business strategy without having to hire a social media manager.

If you're using Wordpress as your CMS tool, the first thing you want to do is search their site for available plugins. You will see they offer a variety you can download (for free), which will automatically post anything (that you post to your website) directly to your social media pages. Pretty cool, right?

If you're looking for an even bigger time saver, I suggest you download a tool called Hootsuite off the internet. If you've never heard of it, it helps you manage your social media pages. I use it all the time and think it's one of the best social media management tools out there. It's really easy and inexpensive to operate, think something in the tune of a cup a coffee (per month), and you get the idea. Hootsuite lets you login into their interface, and you are immediately connected to *all of your social media profiles at once*. This lets you manage everything in one place, which is huge.

Want to know the best part? You can totally automate the process on Hootsuite. You don't have to send out every social media post manually like you're living in the Dark Ages of 2005. All you have to do is create an Excel document with all of your social media content on it, as well as the date you want the content posted, and upload it to Hootsuite, and just like that, they post them for you.

Say you want a "Happy Holidays" post to go out to all of your followers on all of your social media pages. You can set that request up months in advance in Hootsuite. Or let's say you are interested in setting up multiple posts that you want to go out (daily) across all your social media channels for a month. You can set that all up in Hootsuite ahead of time then you don't have to worry about it.

Now, if you think the idea of posting daily is overkill: think again. A steady stream of posts is standard operating procedure for many big businesses. As you might imagine, many big companies have put a lot of research into how to best leverage social media, and the consensus is frequent posts are good because they help awaken your social network. The same thing goes for your blog so don't be afraid to put yourself out there daily (or multiple times a day), as long as you have something to say. It doesn't matter who your audience is, you have to keep your fan base engaged, and fresh posts is one great way to do it.

Get In the Conversation

Another amazing way to build a grassroots fan base is to engage with other people and "get in the conversation." What does "jumping in the conversation" even mean? It simply means you reply to people who are talking about issues related to your internet business. There is a famous saying about making the most out of your social media interactions, which is, "If you play in their sandbox, they will play in yours." Translated, that means if you want people to respond, forward or like your posts – then you need to reciprocate, by responding, forwarding and liking their posts.

Don't try to recreate the wheel now that you know how it works. Just play the game! You really can't be passive in the social media world, you need to get your hands dirty and play in other people's sandboxes if you want to build a network of loyal followers who will do the same for you.

The good news is Hootsuite is a great dashboard for getting in the conversation. How so? You need be on top of current events in order to say anything intelligent to anyone, so how do you do stay current? In Step Thirteen, I mentioned setting up Google Alerts, which works great, but you can also tag certain keywords that relate to your business in Hootsuite — so when those keywords come up in other people's posts, you are immediately notified and can jump in the conversation *fast*.

If you can engage people in an informed dialogue, then eventually others will start to view you as a social media "influencer" in your field. And that's what you want to be, a subject matter expert on whatever it is you do best. So get out there, and if you can perform all of these simple tasks and make the most of your social media platforms, trust me, all your hard work will drive more likes, followers (and attention) your way and help build a relevant audience around your business.

Make Your Content Fun And Engaging

I know you're a business, but that doesn't mean you have to be boring! When posting anything to social media, remember to make your content as fun and engaging as possible. Rarely does content "go viral" that is dull so make it interesting, will ya? What if your business is just not that interesting? C'mon, don't be negative! People love pretty pictures so (at least) try to include some compelling images or videos in your posts.

Want to know a great way to ensure that you get a ton of views? Try embedding a popular video on your blog. Isn't that theft? Like I explained, you can repurpose "existing content" into "original content" by simply writing your own opinion of the popular video in your blog post, and suddenly it's an original piece of content. Just make sure you properly source the videos that you share. You may think this is cheating, but a lot of reputable businesses do it, so if it's within the rules, why not leverage what works?

And believe me, it does. When people start sharing that viral video you just posted, guess what they're really doing? They're sharing your site with thousands of new people. Did you see what I just did? I just gave you a secret to getting millions of likes and followers! And this trick is "low hanging fruit" no less, which means it takes very little time to put together.

What's not to like about that?

STEP FIFTEEN:

OPTIMIZE YOUR WEBSITE FOR SEO

"Content is king, but marketing is queen, and runs the household."
— *Gary Vaynerchuk*

Now that you have your business site and social media pages fully operational, let's talk about how you can rise to the top of Google's search rankings. Here's a little secret: if you're in the proverbial "Google gutter" when it comes to your site rankings, your business won't even have the chance to reach a wide audience.

Why? Because no one will know you exist.

Owning an amazing site with substandard SEO is like creating a great product and only selling it on the "dark side of the moon." What's the point if no one is going to see it? If you want your internet business to soar, you have to get it "out there" where everyone can discover how amazing it is.

One popular way is through SEO, which, if you recall from Step Four, is the process of raising your site's visibility on Google. Ranking high in an organic search result can make a business millions of dollars, which is why everyone jockeys to get their site as highly ranked as possible.

I know what you're asking: how should I optimize my site so I'm setting my business up for success? It's an interesting question I hear all the time. Maybe it's because I own more than a thousand websites, but people love to ask me, "What is the secret to having great SEO?" I like to tell them, " If you ever meet a so-called SEO expert who tells you they can make a SEO miracle happen for your business overnight, RUN. There is no secret, trick or quick fix that will instantly skyrocket your site to the top. Stick to the fundamentals."

In other words, you have to do it the old-fashioned way, and earn it. I hope you followed my advice from Step Four and included (at least) one commonly searched keyword in your domain name. If you did, you're in excellent position to climb the search engine results ladder even if you do no SEO. Why?

Search engines crawl the web looking for keywords that match the searcher's keyword query. They love finding exact keyword matches in domain names. If you have one in your business/domain title, the Google Bots can easily find your site, which will help you rise faster among your competitors. Now, if you started an internet business that *does not* have a popular keyword in your domain name, don't worry; you're not sunk. Yes, it will take a little longer for your site to climb all the way to the top, but it can be done. How? Geez, do you want me to divulge all of my SEO secrets?

Just kidding, I know you're itching to learn as much as you can but let's not get ahead of ourselves. We can't overlook the most obvious way to get eyeballs on your website, which is don't skimp on your site content. *The best way to rank higher in Google has nothing to do with SEO and everything to do with building an engaging site that has a constant stream of new rich content, which adds value to the end user.*

If you can do that, over time, Google will take notice and your site will begin to rise naturally.

Cultivate Your Link Garden

Another fundamental tip to building SEO is to link your site to outside sites (through repurposed content or via fresh blog stories that contain links). It's another easy way for Google to recognize your site without doing any advanced SEO on your end.

You may notice that I'm stressing the SEO fundamentals here (like creating fresh content and building links); I'm doing it because these moves will stand the test of time. Sure, there are quick fix "tricks" out there that will temporarily boost your SEO rankings but none of them will last, why?

Because Google got smart.

Few people remember, when Google was created back in 1998, the largest factor in their ranking algorithm was the number of sites links you have. Even though Google's algorithm has gotten more complex over the years, link building remains one of the most important factors to having a high search ranking. Smart webmasters have found ways to game the system, but Google fought back with random algorithm changes that weeded out the hackers and their sneaky little SEO tricks. That is why you have to do things the right way if you want your work to last.

All Links Are Not Created Equal

While you are cultivating your link garden, remember that all links are not created equal. The best links come from credible and relevant websites. Let's say your internet business focuses on collecting baseball cards. Links from other credible baseball sites (like ESPN.com or MLB.com) will add the most value to your Google ranking. That means if you post a link to your site from one of the "heavy hitters" in your field, it will yield much more value than links from less credible sites.

Be sure to stay away from linking to sites that are not logically related to what you do. If you link your baseball card collecting site to a bunch of orchid collecting sites, for example – you're just going to confuse Google, and the link will not have as much value in their eyes. *Stick to what you know.*

Linking to other sites is not enough. You also need to convince other websites to link to your site. How do you do this? It has nothing to do with technology; it's called Public Relations, folks! You have to reach out to the site owners and establish a relationship with them. Keep in mind, you're not just building a business, you're also building a professional network at the same time. Reaching out to like-minded websites (you respect) is a great way to do this. You will make friends with people in your industry and slowly begin to "get in the conversation" as an "influencer" in your industry.

I suggest you find several sites you admire, which are in the same industry as your business, and ask the owner if they will become "link-friends" with your site. Don't be shy. I've found if you support their site, they will often find a way to support yours.

The Importance of Clear Anchor Text

If you've already found a partner site who wants to be your link-friend, great job! Be sure the links they create are titled clearly. The Google Bots need as much help as they can get to properly navigate web surfers to the sites they're interested in – so make it easy for them. Ideally, you want the Google Bots to be able to read several keywords in the link (otherwise known as "anchor text") so your site can "get in the game" quickly and begin to build some SEO momentum.

Let's say an outside site links to your baseball card collecting site with the link "baseball card collector." That is clearly written anchor text, which will give your site a better chance of ranking higher when people search Google for "baseball card collectors." If the link is not clearly written, then the Google Bots will have a hard time categorizing your site as an influencer in the world of baseball card collecting.

See what I mean? The Google Bots love precision.

I wish that was it ... but there is so much more to having great SEO. Learning the nuances can get extremely technical so I'm not going to attempt to explain everything in the short time I have with you. Just know you can go as deep down the SEO rabbit hole, as you want. I could teach you a bunch of technical SEO tricks like "canonical tags" to add to your site, but I don't think that will be the most useful to you.

My goal here is not to transform you into a SEO genius overnight; I simply want to help you understand the basics so you become a well-rounded internet marketer who builds a great domain that will make money online. If you really want to delve further into technical SEO, I suggest you buy a book that is solely dedicated SEO or hire a SEO professional.

Google Webmaster Tools

Frankly, anything after what I've already shared falls into the category of "technical SEO." What do some of the advanced tricks do? You're curious; I like that! Ok, I'll give you one more tip. You can train your site (through coding) to get friendly with the Google Bots so you *inspire them to crawl your site more often*. First, you must sign up for something called *Google Webmaster Tools,* which is an interface you can use to help boost your site rankings.

You can use *Google Webmaster Tools* to tell Google where your sitemap XML file lives on your site. *This is hugely important.* Your XML file is your site blueprint that lists all of your web pages. The clearer you are about how your site is constructed, the easier it will be for Google to navigate your site. Your XML sitemap will also regularly update Google on all the changing pages on your site, which allows Google to find your pages much faster.

If I'm getting too technical with all this XML talk, don't flip out. Wordpress has the tools you need to help build and automate your sitemap. There are also tons of free sitemap generators that can build your sitemap to submit to Google. Just make sure Google has your XML sitemap, one-way or the other.

Google Webmaster Tools has other important features like checking if your website is mobile friendly, which is very important now that more people search on mobile devices than desktop computers – as well as showing you how many search queries Google does for your website. I *strongly urge* you to spend a lot of time exploring all the features of Google Webmaster Tools.

Google Updates

As I briefly mentioned, over the past 20 years, I have been fortunate enough to own more than a thousand websites. In that time, I've experienced everything you can imagine with Google SEO algorithm updates. Some of my sites were built on a house of cards, and were scuttled by stormy weather when Google rolled out one of their many algorithm changes, like Google Penguin or Google Panda. But I learned from my mistakes and went on to build a bunch of sites with great SEO that (not only) survived a Google update – but thrived when our competitors fell by the wayside. Though a lot of trials and errors, I discovered a winning SEO blueprint that I believe will help your internet business navigate through any future Google update. Want to know what my blueprint for SEO success is?

Winning sites who survive Google updates have a sound site structure, fast load time, good site engagement (i.e. users spend a good amount of time on your site), a good social media presence, lots of fresh, rich quality content, Google webmaster integrations, a good mobile user experience and high quality backlinks.

Conversely, websites that see their SEO drop dramatically after a Google algorithm update also share a few characteristics that you definitely want to avoid. Losing sites *have way too many ads, are not mobile friendly, have thin content that is not frequently updated, and too many links from low-quality sites.*

If I can give you any advice, it's pattern your business site after the *former* and not the *latter*. Now that you have my SEO blueprint, there is no excuse for failure! I want you to build your site strong, right out of the gate. Learn from my mistakes. Practice the fundamentals that I laid out here and follow these simple SEO rules, and I promise you will be on your way to having a technically sound website (with great search rankings) that can weather any storm.

STEP SIXTEEN:

"OLD SCHOOL" PRESS RELEASES

"Without publicity, a terrible thing
happens. *Nothing.*"
— *P.T. Barnum*

Since I've been working in the technology industry, one thing I've noticed is a lot of young web entrepreneurs I meet have no idea how to promote their business if it isn't done on MailChimp or social media. Maybe it's the millennial generation's collective love for their iPhones, but there are other "old school" public relations tools that young entrepreneurs seem to have disregarded these days – big mistake.

I get that you want your PR and marketing campaigns to be cutting edge, but if you also want your message to reach other influencers in the business world, consider leveraging some of the more traditional PR channels that cater strictly to businesses. I'm not suggesting a PR/marketing campaign on Facebook, Twitter, or even Snapchat is unprofessional or ineffective – all I'm saying is can you mix LinkedIn in there somewhere?

The point is to use these *old school Public Relations tools* to get your message out to segments of our society who may not be on social media. I'm talking about the Baby Boomers and Gen Xers who have accumulated the most resources in the United States, so you probably want them buying or at least knowing about what you are selling, right?

But going old school with your PR is not just about reaching an audience who's in a higher tax bracket – it's also about beating your competition for audience mindshare. Think about it: most people use social media primarily for entertainment, which means, if you use those platforms exclusively to promote your business then you will be competing with a virtual fire hose of non-stop static, fluff and noise for the attention of you audience. Why not find a channel that isn't so crowded? Why not target your messages through some traditional PR channels that are proven to be effective? I know, I'm kinda starting to sound like my Dad, but it's true!

All Hail The Old School Press Release

One old school PR method is the tried and true *press release*. Yes, the simple press release that your great-great-grandfather could have used to promote his andiron business back in 1917 is still a great way to ensure you will have some pretty powerful eyeballs following what your internet business is doing.

Press releases are usually one-page stories about a business that (if they are timely, interesting and well written) get picked up by news organizations and hopefully re-printed in their (usually online) publications as "business news." Attention from the traditional media is one of the strongest ways to build credibility for your internet business.

Trust me – being able to showcase your press clippings on your site (and show them off to potential new clients) can often be "the" difference maker when it comes to landing or keeping a new big customer account.

Don't Underestimate the Power of the Media

We all know the media gets a bad rap – forget about it. It doesn't matter what you think of the traditional media's supposed biases, don't under-estimate their power. The media can get your business massive exposure and be an amazingly helpful – just ask Donald Trump! The media played a huge role in helping him shock the world; he got billions of dollars of free press through the traditional media (not to mention social media where he basically owned Twitter). Whether it was good or bad press didn't matter – he was constantly in the news, which helped explode his fan base in ways Twitter alone could not. "The Donald" even credited (social) and traditional media for winning the election for him in an interview with *60 Minutes*. I'm telling you, if it can work for the guy in the White House, it can work for you.

I'm not saying to throw out your social media PR campaigns – I want you to complement your social media marketing with old school methods like sending out press releases as early and often as possible. You want your business to be mentioned on as many reputable sites as you can, so by sending out a constant stream of well-written, content-rich press releases – guess what? You will have easily added your business name (and a link to your site) to a slew of credible web sites across the web. That is huge.

How do you actually create a press release?

Don't worry all you tech addicts – *you can create a press release completely online*. I know, "Phew," right? You don't even have to leave the house, talk to a living person, or kill a tree in order to create one.

There are a ton of online tools and PR agencies out there (if you have the budget to hire an agency) that can help you get your business mentioned in top publications. If you're not there yet financially, get in the habit of issuing "artisanal hand-crafted" press releases that you create yourself, early and often. Just make sure you have something relevant to say or no one will pick up your press release.

I personally would not worry about hiring an expensive PR firm at this stage of your business – you can easily do it yourself with a tool like PRWeb.com. I use it and think it's a great way to get all your PR press releases published in all the traditional web media sources, often *overnight*. I've seen press releases posted on PRWeb.com get picked up by large websites like Yahoo – give them a shot, you may find your press release on *Yahoo Finance*, which would be awesome exposure, no matter what business you are in.

And even if a big media outlet does not pick up your press release, don't fret. I've never seen a press release generated from PRweb.com not show up in an organic Google search for your business.

Which leads me to another big benefit of issuing press releases. It's not just about attracting influential eyeballs to your site – every press release that is picked up or mentioned on other reputable sites will also help improve your site's *overall SEO*. That's right, press releases not only help you get exposure from influencers in your field, it also helps boost your organic search volume to your website. What's not to like about that?

So start using press releases, I can't promise they alone will automatically get your business mentioned in *The Wall Street Journal* – or propel your website to a #1 search ranking on Google – but generating a continual flow of solid press releases is a great addition to your PR and SEO strategy.

STEP SEVENTEEN:

SECURITY, CREDIBILITY, & PRIVACY

"I think computer viruses should count as
life. It says something about human
nature that the only form of life
we have created so far is purely
destructive. We created life
in our own image."
– *Stephen Hawking*

You may remember my horror story from Step Two when Russian hackers tried to take down one of my first sites called *WallpaperPimper*. I bring that incident back up for good reason – as someone who has been through numerous internet attacks, you have to be diligent about preventing them from the moment you launch your site. I don't want to scare you (actually I do, it's for your own good) but *your entirely livelihood is at stake here*. You're not too small to fly under the radar; no one is. It may sound like a script from a Tom Clancy novel, but hackers want to destroy your internet business; they are out there waiting to disable your site or steal your sensitive information right now. Don't let them. Be smart and fight back.

As we witnessed during the U.S. Presidential election, web security is one of the largest issues (if not the biggest one) affecting everyone on the internet today. There are so many tricks out there to steal data and information, it's vitally important that you have a plan to protect your internet business. If Russian hackers can influence the outcome of a U.S. Presidential election by hacking into private emails and posting them on *Wikileaks* – someone can surely hack your website, so get your guard up.

I'm not exaggerating when I say that it's not a question of *if* it will happen, but how will you respond when it does? Here are some of the most popular methods hackers are using these days – get them on your radar so you can protect your business against them.

SQL Injections

This is one of the most common forms of internet attacks; *SQL injection* is not like a digital version of botox, it's a code that can be injected into your site through an *online form* that you have on your site. Just putting a form online that could potentially access your site's database (with no security protection) is an extremely bad idea – don't do it.

If you are building your site yourself, I recommend you use a plugin called *Captcha* (for Wordpress) to prevent these attacks. If you're working with a developer, have them setup security precautions to guard against SQL injection attacks.

Limit Characters In Online Forms

Here is a precaution any developer can take to guard against an SQL injection. If you have an online form on your site – your developer should make sure that each data entry point on the form (called fields) do not allow for an unlimited number of characters to be entered. Leaving an unlimited amount opens up a ton of computer code that a hacker can submit to your website in order to try to break in.

Say you have an online form where a customer can enter in his or her address. Limit the characters that can be entered in that field to a reasonable amount of keystrokes.

If you can afford it, I strongly suggest you hire a professional to help secure your site, especially if your entire livelihood hinges on your site never going down – because if you aren't diligent about fighting hackers, one day when you least expect it, a sneaky little SQL Injection will suddenly paralyze your internet business like a bad Botox injection from hell.

That "deer in the headlights" face doesn't look good on anyone.

Stay A Step Ahead of Password Hacking

We hear a lot about password theft today because it's happening everywhere, all the time. It should go without saying that it's a great idea to make a habit of consistently updating your FTP passwords (or Wordpress login) to keep the bad people out. I mean a lot. Most importantly, you have to consistently update your password for "Root" access to your site; this is like the "self destruct" button on the *Death Star* if a hacker gets into it, so guard it with your life.

Once a hacker gets into your site through your Root access password, they can visit anything that is stored on your server. For your internet business, this situation is akin to NORAD taking the United States to Defcon 1 – so guard all your passwords like they are gates to your castle but especially your Root password.

If a hacker gets their sweaty little hands on your Root password, your fully functional site will be blown to bits like the Death Star right before your eyes.

Comment Spamming

Comment section spamming may seem like no big deal to the casual web user, but it's a real problem for site owners since (again), it has to do with an online *form field*. Limit custom comment posting on your site; I prefer that you use a *comment posting tool* like my favorite, the *Facebook comment application*, which allows users on your site to post their comments directly to Facebook, which remove your site from the equation.

Sounds like a pretty good deal, right? Let Facebook deal with the comment spamming issue and focus your time on protecting your site in other ways.

Have A Strong Privacy Policy From Day One

Don't wait until you have been compromised to create a good "privacy policy" and "terms and conditions" for your site. Get ahead of the game on this. Steadfastly protecting your user's information has to be one of your internet business's key foundational values, or you won't be in business very long.

Try adding a *security lock symbol* to your site with a note about how you keep information secure, along with a *link to your privacy policy* that details exactly how your business keeps your information secure. Showcasing the steps you've taken will not scare customers away – just the opposite actually – doing so will only increase your site's user interaction and conversion rate.

Got An E-Commerce Site? Use SSL Certificates

If you're running an e-commerce site, you have even more responsibility to protect your customer's private information. You have to have the right tools in place to ensure your customers' credit card information is safe of you will have zero credibility and no one will trust your site. You should start by getting a "SSL Certificate" for your e-commerce site, it will turn your website from a http:// to an https:// – the added "s" indicates to web consumers that your site is secure.

After you have gotten your SSL Certificate, you can apply for a *secure seal (from Norton or Symantec)* for your site, which will prove to the world that your site is secure. This is not some dog and pony show where you are giving yourself some frivolous award – no, you earned this one. That *seal of approval* will ultimately give your site more legitimacy in your industry, which will thereby increase your websites performance. Can you see how *security* leads to *legitimacy* – which leads to helping your bottom line?

Take it from someone who has been on the wrong side of this "hacking issue" a few times in my career – don't skimp on your site security, even if you think you are too small to need it. Using the right type of site security, then clearly showcasing your *secure site seal* and your *privacy policy* on your site will only earn you more *credibility* from your customers.

Customers today absolutely want to know your business cares about their privacy. In a web that is filled with so many untrustworthy websites – why not be one of the trusted ones who offers a safe sanctuary for all of your customer's private information? If you can offer them a site that sells a great product or service, works like a charm and also is verifiably secure, they will trust you with their business, and keep coming back for more – and that's the goal of any business, no matter what industry you are in.

STEP EIGHTEEN:

LEARN FROM YOUR COMPETITION

'Only a fool learns from his mistakes. The wise person learns from the mistakes of others."
– *Otto Van Bismark*

Has "everything" been done on the internet? No way, the tech world is just getting warmed up when it comes to innovating on the web, which should be music to your ears if you're planning on "breaking the internet" with your totally new business idea – but let's get real for a minute. If you're like the vast majority of entrepreneurs who jump in the tech game, you may currently think you're doing something totally unique, but the odds are good that you have started an internet business that has already been done (or at least attempted) before by someone, somewhere.

Don't go taking a long walk down a short bridge just because you aren't the first to do it. It would be awesome if we all had the next Snapchat in our back pockets – but here's a little secret: *taking an existing idea and making it even better* is a great position to be in as an internet entrepreneur. There is no shame in being second to market; in many cases, I'd personally rather be second than first – what do I mean?

Ever heard the old maxim, "Pioneers usually die of bugs and dysentery?" It's so true, especially in the tech world. "Second movers" tend to have much better success than the person who was first to market with a new web product or service. There are plenty of stories of tech entrepreneurs who took a good existing idea and made it amazing (think: Facebook after seeing MySpace). Mark Zuckerberg didn't go all "Lewis & Clark" on some undiscovered country of an idea – he sat back and watched how MySpace did it, then said, "Good idea. I think I can do it better."

If you are the second (or even the 20th) person to start your particular type of internet business, look around at your competition and learn from the first pioneer's mistakes. Your successful competitors will show you what works, and your not-so-successful ones will show you what doesn't.

Even if you're leading the pack to market on some unfathomable new product that literally has never been done before – don't adopt the mindset of a Formula 1 driver in "pole position" who never looks in his rearview mirror because "What's behind me isn't important." Trust me, what's behind you, around you, and especially in front of you – is extremely important! You can always do it better, faster, smarter, with better functionality and better customer service – so don't get cocky and keep your eyes peeled.

Study your competition like the livelihood of your big business dream depends on it, because it does. Web entrepreneurs who patiently watch (and learn) are usually the most successful – so feel free to copy a competitor's moves if they are doing something better than you. I'm not saying steal corporate secrets, but there are ways to emulate a successful competitor without breaking any laws, especially on the internet where you can learn a lot simply by clicking around your competitors' websites.

Tools To Help You Research Your Competition

When it comes to driving visitors to *your* website, there is no better place to get ideas than by researching your competition. The good news is you don't have to do all the research yourself. There are a lot of websites out there that can help you learn more your competition. Here are a few that will help you research your competition's site traffic and marketing campaigns – so your business ends up in the pole position, no matter whether your business was the first or the 20th to enter the race.

1. **Alexa.com** – Amazon recently acquired Alexa.com, which you may only know as just *Alexa* if you've seen the commercials. After watching the ads, you might think Alexa is just a Siri for Amazon Echo, not so – Alexa is a great resource for all internet entrepreneurs even if you haven't bought an Echo – Alexa provides extremely useful customer information on your web competitors. How does "she" do it? Alexa has installed millions of browser toolbars (to millions of websites) over the years, so

she has great insight into how much traffic your competition is getting (and where it is coming from). Alexa will also provide you with "directional data" that shows you exactly who and what is driving traffic to your competitor's website. So setup an Alexa account today and analyze the clickstream that is driving all that traffic to your competitors' websites. It will be very revealing, I guarantee.

    a. **Reddit** – Here is a good example of what I mean: Let's say Alexa says 95% of your competition's traffic is driven by Reddit users, which is a web content rating and discussion site, among other things – what do you do with this information? Start a blanket marketing campaign that targets all Reddit users? Perhaps if you can afford it, you may find out after you've done your customer research that you should "test market" your business on a few different platforms like Reddit. But before you take any action, keep digging. Search Reddit to find out what is driving traffic to your competitors. Once you do, you can then a) Get into the Reddit conversation that is causing the steady stream of customers to your competitor's website or b) See how your competition is marketing their site on Reddit and copy their moves.

2. **SEMRush.com** – SEMRush.com allows you to run "keyword reports" to determine what keywords drive the most traffic to your website as well as to your competitors. SEMRush will help you determine what percentage of your site traffic (or your competitor's site traffic) comes through SEO and

organic search results, versus traffic that's coming through SEM (search engine marketing) or paid search results.

3. **Moat.com** – Another piece of valuable "intel" is to uncover what advertising campaigns your competitors are running. Moat.com is a great resource for doing just that; it archives most of the "display ads" we see on the web. If you simply search your competitor's domain name on Moat, you can see all the display ads that are used by your competitors on the web. This is valuable information because it reveals your competitor's ad partners. Once you know who your competitors are working with, you can differentiate your marketing campaigns from your competitors' – and if you discover a tactic you can transfer to your own marketing campaign without stealing any corporate secrets, I say go for it. All is fair in love and war!

4. **Ghostery.com** – Another great way to discover what kind of advertising your competitors are using is to leverage a site like Ghostery.com, which allows you to add an extension to your browser that will show all the "computer code tags" on your competitors' websites. This is important information because tags will often clue you into secrets like the keywords that are being used in your competitor's current advertising campaigns. That's another piece of crucial intelligence!

Ignorance is not bliss in the technology world. The more you know the better luck you will have. So do your due diligence when researching your competition – put on your spy hat and find out what you are up against; leverage the resources that I listed above, and don't forget to visit your competitor's websites and landing pages yourself to see what nuggets you can glean. I'm telling you, a simple eye test will yield some very interesting findings that you can also use as valuable weapons against your competition.

And don't break any corporate espionage laws unless you want to start a second career as a Russian hacker.

STEP NINETEEN:

START MAKING MONEY FROM YOUR SITE

'The best way to make happy money is to
make money your hobby
and not your god."
– *Scott Alexander*

The moment has finally arrived – now that your internet business is armed with an amazing amount of data on your competition – you have a pretty good idea of what your competitors are doing, right? Congratulations. Feels good to do your homework doesn't it? Now it's time to start making money from your internet business, how exciting is that? Getting through the first 18 Steps of my book is an impressive accomplishment, but as my Dad used to wisely say to me (every time I asked him for some pocket money), "Money doesn't grow on trees, son." No, Dad, money doesn't grow on trees, but guess what? It does grow on the internet!

My goal for Step Nineteen is to teach you to add as many profit arms (or profit streams) to your internet business as possible so you always have a steady income stream. I've noticed a lot of entrepreneurs these days only set up on one or two profit streams for their business, which is crazy. What happens when that profit arm is not pulling its weight? You're sunk, right? Not if you have other profit arms that can pick up the slack – so what are your options?

I know this may sound unbelievable to a lay person, but there really are only six ways to make money from your website. Do you want to know what they are?

6 Ways To Make Money On The Internet

1. **Advertising Revenue** – This is the classic "profit stream" that even the old school print newspapers (used to) live by. Advertising money for an internet business (however) is not generated from newspaper sales, it comes from the amount of "user views or clicks" on an ad that appears on your website – either on your desktop, mobile app, or a video ad (on your website) or a partner site. Advertising revenue can also be earned in a number of different ways like paid advertorials, site sponsorships, and newsletter

sponsorships, or payment for inclusion in your website or social media platform. If you can attract advertising revenue to your site, it's a no-brainer.

2. **Google Adsense** – While we're on the topic of ad revenue, it's important to know about Google Adsense, which is, hands down, the best way to start making money from your blog or website. Now that you're driving traffic to your website in a number of ways, you will continue to see your organic traffic rise (over time) if you continue to follow the practices outlined in this book. The way Google Adsense works is very simple, Google provides you with a small snippet of code to place on your web pages. This code will automatically search Google's database of advertisers and display a relevant ad on your site right next to your content. Let's say you write a blog post about skin care. You may see an ad from the largest brands like Olay or Estee Lauder right next to your content. The best part is that whenever a user clicks on their ad, you will immediately get paid a cost per click! Per click payments can range from .05 cents all the way up to $20 or $30 per click in some categories. Adsense is also very easy to use, the code they provide will display ads that are responsive, which means they work on any sized screen, including mobile devices and iPads. You can even change the color of the ads to match your website design to integrate them further into your website's look, which will help drive more clicks on your ads. Google continues to expand the tools and features it offers to web publishers, so once you get to this step, you'll be on your way to great profits. For my company, we have sites that were built years ago that aren't updated as much, due to other projects, that still generate substantial Adsense revenue. That's one of the best

parts of Adsense — it's can be a great source of passive income for years to come.

3. **Subscription Revenue** — Subscription revenues are funds that are paid to your company in order to subscribe to a continual product or service you offer. Are you selling any product or service that is constantly being used? Then you can probably set up subscription revenue; it can be anything from a curated box of goods, to a yearly "club" to receive a monthly software or technology subscription. Again if you can add this profit arm to your business, then you should surely do it.

4. **Transaction Revenue** — Transaction revenue is exactly what it sounds like — it is "funds paid for the purchase of a product or service on your website." If you are an ecommerce site, naturally this is one of the primary ways you will make money. You can also have other profit streams but when you are selling a product or a service, this will probably be your biggest revenue source.

5. **Affiliate Revenue** — This is an, "I scratch your back, you scratch mine" *quid pro quo* situation set up between partnering companies (called affiliates) who have some arrangement that allows them to work together to drive customer traffic to each other's websites. If you are already driving traffic to an affiliate company's website for whatever reason, don't do it for free. Contact the owner of that site and see if you can establish an agreement where you can get paid for doing something you may already be doing for free. Don't just reach out to one business, reach out to all the other web businesses who may be fishing in the same pond as you are, and see if you can set up some

"affiliate revenue" agreements that will help both of your businesses attract new customers.

6. **Data Revenue** – Data revenue is money you earn by selling customer information to a third-party website. This fairly common practice has gotten a lot of negative attention in the news lately for all the wrong reasons. People are (rightly) concerned about companies like Facebook, Google, and Apple sharing client data with other companies (and ahem our federal government) – but it's a legit (all legal) way to make money on the internet, that is why so many web owners do it. If you are going to add data revenue to your site's profit stream, I suggest you appropriately communicate the fact that your site shares certain information with outside parties so you are being totally transparent to your users.

Which Model Fits Your Business?

Now that you know about your six options for revenue generation, ask yourself, which revenue model best fits my internet business? Feel free to experiment with all six if your business is set up that way. The goal is to get all of your business's profit arms in place as quickly as possible so you can begin earning your first dollar. Sounds like a piece of cake, right? *Earning your first dollar is going to be the hardest buck you will ever earn on the internet.* Lots of trial and error usually goes into figuring it all out – but once you have a clear idea of how you can generate revenue through multiple profit streams, and you finally earn that first dollar, you will be well on your way to earning boat loads of tens, twenties, hundreds and (yes) even thousand dollar bills – and those look good in any wallet.

STEP TWENTY:

PARTNER WITH RELEVANT SITES IN YOUR FIELD

"Build it, and they will come'
only works in the movies."
— Seth Godin, Entrepreneur

Ever see that old baseball movie, *Field of Dreams*? The famous quote from the movie is, "If you build it, they will come." This notion may have been true for crazy Kevin Costner who built a baseball diamond on his Iowa cornfield for ghosts of old ballplayers to play on but is it true for an internet business site?

Does site traffic ever just come out of the corn?

It doesn't happen that way in real life – sorry magic fans. I know the underdog Cubs and Red Sox recently won the World Series, but don't push your luck! Dreams like that don't come true in the business world unless you do a lot more than simply hope for the best under the pale moonlight. "IRL" (In Real Life) for just about every person who has ever built a successful internet business means that you have to drive traffic with more than a marketing slogan – but how?

This is one of the most popular questions I get from young entrepreneurs I meet. Let me offer you some sound advice, it doesn't matter how amazing your business is, you can't do it alone. Repeat after me: *"If you partner, they will come."* Partnerships make the world go around, especially on the internet.

Now that you're learning how to monetize your site, I want you to spend some time *identifying a handful of potential allies* in the business world. Look for websites you admire; they can be *business sites, blogs, news sites* – even *social media* or *entertainment sites* (if they do what you do). Don't be shy. Reach out to sites in your own "personal field of dreams" and tell them how much you like what they do (here's a hint: flattery never hurts when trying to get in the door). Then see if you can start a dialogue with them – and potentially work together. Work with them on what – you ask? On building a fan base and making money of course!

That's what all this is about – right?

I don't want you to play a leisurely game of catch with them, I want you to learn to play together so you can help each other score some runs, which, in the business world means attracting paying customers. Keep in mind, every relationship doesn't have to pay monetary dividends immediately. Any partnership you make (with a reputable URL) will help you build momentum in the long run. So get out there and test the waters, make yourself known – see what partnership interest you can generate.

Just like meeting new people in real life, there are an infinite number of ways to set up an online business partnership. Since I don't have time to explain them all in this book, let's focus on the three most common partnerships – which are advertising partnerships, content partnerships, and link partnerships.

Advertising Partnerships

In most cases, the best way to get a relevant site's attention is to buy advertising on their site – duh. Money talks loudest of all in the world of commerce, it always has. But don't start "making it rain" like a drunken sailor on shore leave just because you find a pretty site that catches your eye. Be strategic about those sites you invest in with real advertising dollars.

I suggest you find several "relevant websites" to your field of dreams that have potential to be good partners, then be sure to test every advertising opportunity "for performance." *Research how to get the biggest bang for your advertising dollar.* You don't want to put all your marketing eggs in one basket – so shop around. Remember, building a strong presence *across many relevant sites in your category* is valuable to any business in the long run – so spread your love around, and buy advertising on several sites if you have the marketing budget for that.

Of course, not everyone has those kind of marketing resources just lying around. So let's say you only have the resources to advertise on one site – *pick the most relevant site with the biggest audience.* Once you have identified the site you want to place advertising on (with hopes of aligning your brand with theirs) — here are the four most common metrics (or pricing methods) used when buying internet advertising:

1) Cost Per Impression — Usually for every 1,000 impressions or site views

2) Cost Per Click — A fixed cost for every click on your ad

3) Flat Sponsor Rate — A flat fee for each piece of ad space purchased

4) Revenue Sharing — Shares the money you make off the traffic driven to your site, from the ad you bought on their site.

I listed these methods above in order of highest to lowest risk — with *Cost Per Impression* being the riskiest form of advertising — and *Revenue Sharing*, being, as you might imagine, the least risky way to buy advertising, since you are only paying a percentage of the "future profits" you make off the advertising itself — kind of like when you share the "future profits" of selling (say) a vintage coat at a consignment store, with the store who sells it for you. Are you still with me? Great!

Every internet business is different so I want you to test these four different cost structure models to see which advertising buying method works best for you. If I can give you any personal advice — it's *tread carefully* if you decide to go with a *Cost Per Impression* or *Cost Per Click* model. Novice ad buyers may assume that you can just buy "Cost for Impression or Click" ad space, drop it over the fence and expect the ad to grow into the ground like a magic bean from Kevin Costner's magic cornfield. Not true.

You have to nurture your seed ad investment by "keeping your eye on the ball" at all times, to ensure it is working. Make sure you are measuring your analytics (daily) to check their site's performance. Don't let anyone tell you the site traffic metrics; monitor it yourself! You need to be certain that you are paying the correct rate (per click or per impression) for your advertising. Trust me, the people running your partner site will respect you for it in the long run, and be more inclined to partner with you on future projects if they know you are detail-oriented, and seriously in the game.

Content Partnerships

Content partnerships are another excellent way to partner with a site and improve your SEO at the same time. Content partnerships are exactly what they sound like – they all relate to *generating branded content that you will share.* One of the most common types of branded *content partnerships* is when a business (say, like yours) reaches out to a relevant blog that covers your industry, and offers to write an article, do an interview, or provide the blog with some unique content for their site (be it written, video, or audio content) – in exchange for a link to your site at the end of the story (that you created for them).

Sounds like a win-win, right? That is exactly what it is if you partner with the right site. The goal is to create-then-share *branded content* with partnering sites that attract the same type of eyeballs you want to your site. Their audience should naturally be interested in what your business does – use your brain! You don't want to advertise your Hipster Taxidermy site on a vegetarian blog, do you? What would be the point of advertising to people who oppose what you do?

You're not running for president! So use your best judgment to find content partnership opportunities that are natural fits. Never try to sell to the wrong audience. It just doesn't work that way in real life.

Link Partnership

A third type of partnership is called a *link exchange* (or link partnership) – which sounds just like it functions. Here is how it works: Once you've located a relevant site you like and want to partner with, reach out to them, and offer to link your site to theirs (for free) in exchange for a link on their site. This is called reciprocity – quid pro quo, it's been happening since the beginning of time. Don't try to fix what already works! Be aware that, in the not-so-distant-past (i.e. just a few years ago), link exchanges were one of the best ways to increase your SEO rankings on Google.

Oh, how things have changed!

Google decided not to value link partnerships the same way they used to. Why? Devious and diabolical webmasters out in the world were caught ceaselessly trying to use link exchanges to game the system, in order to get better SEO traction. So that little trick doesn't work nearly as well as it once did.

Considering how Google's rules have changed for link partnerships – I believe the best link partnership for your site would be to acquire a "one-way link" on a relevant site (or blog) that links to your website. This way you don't need to link back. As for how you sell your business to that site? That's entirely up to you.

Remember, the higher quality the site, the more valuable that link will be for your site – so aim high. It's important that your site has a lot of sticky new content before asking a blog to link to your site – so keep churning new content and keep trying to acquire links organically, and not through buying them.

If you can get a "one-way link" on a relevant site that attracts the same audience you want for your business, that is the ideal. If not, an "I scratch your back, you scratch mine" two-way link is still helpful to your site growth, even if it doesn't boost your SEO like it once did. Remember, if you are still looking for that old school SEO boost from a link partnership, it's always a good practice to check the link code (of any site you want to link to), and attempt to get a link that doesn't have "rel=nofollow" – why? Google will not add any SEO value to these types of links! You have been warned.

Happy partnership hunting!

STEP TWENTY-ONE:

TRY AFFILIATE MARKETING ON FOR SIZE

"Make your marketing so useful
people would *pay for it.*"
– *Jay Baer*

The act of *doing business* has been around for eons, even before the idea of currency was conceived, cavemen were probably holding yard sales, trading a hundred bearskins to get a summer timeshare at the penthouse cave with the great view of the tar pits. You can probably tell by that comment, I'm no Ken Burns-type historian – but even an amateur like me would wager to bet there has been some business (somewhere) that struck proverbial gold without advertising. Now, has there ever been a successful internet business that eschewed advertising completely?

That's a totally different question: I can't think of one, can you? If you can, don't fool yourself into thinking it is a viable model: a successful business that never advertises is what we call a "unicorn." I hate to break it to you, but unless you have a regal horn jutting out of your forehead, you're business is probably not a unicorn – don't feel bad, neither are any of my businesses!

Point is: don't expect to succeed like a magical animal in this area.

Don't try to change a business model that has worked since the beginning of time. Any entrepreneur who is serious about making their business shine must market their product or service any way they can. It's true that a grassroots word-of-mouth movement can be a powerful thing – but how will you get the word out if you are selling your stuff in a dark, empty room?

I know what you're thinking – *advertising is expensive* – and it typically is, but it doesn't have to be. Have I got your attention?

Are you dying to know how you can buy low-risk, cost-effective marketing that won't cost you an arm and a leg? You came to the right place. For a small business like yours, that may not have the resources to commit to buying ad space on TV, radio, online or in print. I suggest you partner with an outside firm in a practice known as "affiliate marketing." What is it?

Affiliate marketing is like an advertising partnership where the cost (and risk) is mitigated between two parties who agree to share the revenue from the ads in a profit sharing agreement. Affiliate marketing is a great tool for small businesses who want to have a professional marketing campaign without risking their entire budget on an expensive campaign that might bomb.

Want to know how they work? Sure you do, we all want to save money.

Affiliate marketing agencies usually agree to run ads for your internet business (for a discounted price) on their site as well as on their partnering client's sites. Affiliate marketing firms almost always have a different pricing model from traditional ad firms, in that – they earn some kind of sales commission for promoting your company's products. This is the big difference from traditional advertising firms who often charge a lump sum for the entire project.

Not affiliate marketing firms, they usually charge based on a "cost per action" model – which means they may charge you for each individual action they take to promote your company (like, for example, every time they form a lead, make a sale, close a transaction, make a conversion, or generate a product or service download) – they get a little commission. After doing tons of research on this, I believe affiliate partnership are the best (most cost-effective, low-risk) marketing solutions for a small business like yours.

It's not just the agreeable price and low risk that is appealing to web entrepreneurs – you can also monitor the results of your investment. What a concept. Instead of hiring a big advertising firm for a huge fee where you aren't exactly sure where your investment dollars are going – with affiliate marketing, you see exactly how your money is quantifiably translating into results.

I have worked on marketing for hundreds of internet businesses, and this is absolutely one of the best, most cost-friendly ways to grow your business.

Beware: Some Sites Don't Work With Affiliate Marketing Firms

Ok, so now that I've touted the benefits of working with an affiliate marketing partner – there's also a downside you should know. If you have a big time website (like *The New York Times,* for example) that you dream of (one day) advertising on – you may have problems buying ad space if they don't work with affiliate marketing firms.

Trust me, it happens. Some don't. In fact, many don't.

For one reason or another, some sites refuse to work with affiliate marketing firms. Don't ask me why – if I had to guess I'd say it's because some people assume affliliate marketing companies produce smaller ad revenue than big firms – which is true.

But just know – if you really want to advertise on a site that "doesn't work with affiliate marketers" – and you are already working with an affiliate marketer, it's up to you to reach out to that site you covet and negotiate the best deal possible. Why you and not your affiliate marketing partner? This is not the affiliate marketing company's job. They are not usually in the business of lobbying sites that do not want to work with them.

If you want to place an ad on a site that does not work with affiliate marketers, I suggest you ask if you can run a "test ad" on their site for a short amount of time to see how it goes.

This is the only way you can accurately quantify the traffic you get back from an ad to tell if it is a cost-effective investment. If you do buy a "test ad" and find it is worth the investment – you can usually set up an agreement with them, outside of your agreement with the affiliate marketing firm.

Affiliate marketing contracts are not usually exclusive.

Offers and Incentivized Affiliate Programs

Another wrinkle to consider when your limited marketing budget calls for some creativity – is to investigate whether you can develop an *"offer and incentivized affiliate program"* – which is a side business (of sorts) that will supplement your affiliate partnership program.

This may sound complicated and "out of your league," but it really isn't that difficult to understand. Think of it this way: Let's say you hired an affiliate marketing agency to help you enlist sites who will publish your ads, as well as be responsible for the growth of your marketing program. Your affiliate marketing partnering agency could also manage an "affiliate program" you set up (which can do things like promote special offers and work to get your product or service onto even large affiliate platforms like LinkShare or Commission Junction).

You have to think big if you want to be big – but not so big that you blow your budget on a big ad campaign without having the resources to do it! So be smart and realistic when it comes to your initial marketing. If you're savvy about it and can expand your marketing campaign from a strict promotion to a "special offer" where you are offering your customers incentives to buy now, you are giving customers one more reason to pull the trigger on a purchase, while always looking to grow your ad space.

The big upside to all of this is you are doing it for *little risk* and for a *much lower cost* than you would when working with a traditional Madison Avenue ad agency.

Does this sound like a plan to make the most of your advertising dollars? I'm telling you affiliate marketing works. Now get out there and do your homework. See if you can partner with a reputable affiliate marketing agency and come up with a shared vision for your profit sharing agreement and your business's future.

With a partner on board (who has a vested interest in seeing you succeed because they get a piece of the profits) –

you have just expanded your ability to grow exponentially without blowing your entire budget – and that sound like a pretty good thing *no matter what you're selling.*

STEP TWENTY-TWO:

BUILD A ROCK SOLID LANDING PAGE

"People want to be told so badly
what to do, they will
listen to anyone."
— *Don Draper (TVs* Mad Men*)*

Currency is only as good as the paper it's printed on – same goes for advertising campaigns. They are only as good as the site you're advertising on, which means your landing page for all your marketing campaigns better be able to close the sale, or you are in trouble. You can have the best ad campaign in the world, but if the ad takes you to a lousy home page – you just lost all credibility.

This is literally one of the most common mistakes I see (every day, all over the internet) when it comes to internet marketing – a hot shot company will launch an ad campaign without realizing they don't have a super-sticky, rock-solid landing page that is simple to use, and convincing enough to close the deal. You would think our latest generation of tech entrepreneurs would spend a ton of time making sure the "closer page" is doing its job – but so many don't. What the heck is going on here?

I've found many businesses don't even create individual landing pages for their marketing campaigns; are they just lazy? I don't know, but a lot of businesses skip it, opting to have their ads link directly to their homepage. This can be a good strategy but if you ask me, it's a big mistake – unless you have a homepage that is super sales focused and optimized for converting a paid visitor.

Unfortunately, from my experience, most of the homepages I see are not focused on the sale. They are too busy, with far too many options for the user to click on. You can only imagine what this does to a potential customer. Just like when you are frozen in aisle eight of your local supermarket, staring at the 20 choices of peanut butter – too many options can cause confusion, and keep consumers from buying your product. How can a customer buy anything when they don't know which button to push?

How can a business be so shortsighted not to realize this?

Let me give you an example of what I mean: Let's say an e-commerce footwear company is advertising. They want to drive paid visitors to their homepage. But one of their navigation tabs on their homepage is for "Careers" at that company – which has absolutely nothing to do with the customer experience – so tell me: Why is the customer even looking at it? That link to the "careers page" should never be on a marketing landing page. First, it's confusing and second, that space could have been used to help the user find the shoes they wanted.

This may sound like I am nitpicking – but this is extremely vital stuff. Landing page clutter can kill tons of sales; it happens all the time and what a wasted opportunity – do you realize how hard it was just to get that client to click on that link? If you have managed to get a client to your sales page from your advertising, you've got them on the line. You're so close to getting a sale. Don't screw it up by dangling anything other than sales information in front of their faces. Keep it simple.

Keep it straightforward.

Don't get too flashy or you will lose them in the end.

If you are revisiting your landing page right about now, and realizing perhaps you need to clean it up a bit – the first step to condensing it down to its essence, is to decide *what you want your paid visitors to do once* they reach your page? Seems like a pretty obvious question, right? Ok, once you have figured that out, the second step is – only give your site users the tools to do that one thing.

Also pretty simple stuff, which is my entire point!

Your marketing landing page should be *extremely simple to navigate* with nothing but a "call-to-action" to make that sale. After running millions of tests on landing pages over the years, I've found the clean and easy-to-use pages convert sales much better than the flashy cluttered ones.

You have already done the hard part and hooked them with the ad – when it comes to closing the deal, remember, *simplicity sells*.

My Landing Page 7 Commandments

Besides "keeping your landing page clean," when a customer is ready to buy your product or service – there are a few other essential elements that must be in place before he or she will sign on the dotted line. Here are the seven most essential factors that I have found will help your landing pages (and marketing campaigns) be a success, no matter what you are selling.

1. *Credibility* | You want your paid users to feel confident they are on a reputable website that will do what it says it will – so do not hesitate to show off proof of your professionalism, which can include things like *customer testimonials, professional reviews, star ratings, PR content* or even *brand logos.* Any evidence that validates your credibility will only help users feel more confident when sharing their personal information with you – and instilling confidence is huge when making a sale.

2. *Security* | Everyone wants to know they are doing business with a secure site (especially now with Russian hackers all over the news) – so make your users feel confident in their privacy and security by posting evidence of the steps you have taken to ensure your site is safe and secure. This can include verification indicators like *secure symbols, privacy seals, lock symbols,* and of course, you want to have one of these: https:// in front of your URL to prove that you are running a secure site that has SSL certificates. Never skimp on security.

3. *Legitimacy* | You want your users to know how legitimate your site is, so don't be shy and

show off your "bonafides" – like your *Better Business Bureau (BBB) rating*, any awards you have received, as well as *your business mailing address* so customers can see that you exist in real life. All of this helps people know they are dealing with a legitimate company.

4. ***Sense of Urgency*** | People are more inclined to buy what you are selling when they think that "time is running out" on their chances – so build that sense of urgency in your audience. You can increase your user's desire to convert now by creating *limited time offers, discount coupon codes* and *countdowns* to get people buying now, rather than later.

5. ***Seasonality*** | You can also increase your sales conversion rates by creating limited *seasonal, holiday, or weekend offers* – to build a sense of urgency to buy now. If these seasonal offers are clearly noted on the landing page (and not over used so they lose all meaning) – they will help boost your bottom line, guaranteed.

6. ***GeoTargeting*** | It doesn't matter where we were born, we all have tribal tendencies, whether we want to admit it or not – so it's a good idea to target your marketing to specific areas of the country to improve your landing page conversion rate. People like doing business with their neighbors, so act like one! Let them know that your company serves their specific geographic area, and customers will be more inclined to buy from you. Try a targeted approach to your marketing, and be sure to include the targeted customer's city and

state on your landing page so they know you are "one of them."

7. **Ease of Use** | This one is a no-brainer, folks – keep it simple! Users like simplicity, no one enjoys being baffled, so give them what they want. Help them out, guide them, tell them where to look, and what to do in a simple manner – and your sales conversion rates will improve. It's as simple as that.

Conversion Optimization

After you build your amazing landing page for your marketing campaign, the best way to ensure that your ad campaign has continued success is to do "continual A/B testing" or "multivariate landing page testing" to make sure you are converting consistently. This sounds like a question on a NASA astronaut test, I know, but it's as easy as comparing apples to oranges.

I personally would be a billionaire genius like Mark Cuban if I could tell you that a red background on your landing page (instead of a white background) would be more profitable for converting sales for your internet business – but I can't. Not even Mark Cuban could tell you that magical bit of information!

Is it that big of a secret?

Not really, but web surfers are all so different, and the internet still so new (even today) – you never truly know why something is "working" on the internet until you dig in and quantify your theory with some real numbers to back it up. Sure, we can make our best guess based on prior experience, or we could test a series of radical ideas with no numbers to back it up – but who has the time and the money to scattershoot haphazardly like some internet outlaw?

Time is money so I want you to spend yours making educated decisions so are maxing out the amount of sales you are converting. This means you need to do less guessing and more testing. *Lots more.* I can't promise, after all this testing, that you will end up with a landing page that converts 100% of your sales opportunities – but I can say if we feed enough data into a test, the results will always lead you in the right direction.

Here is a perfect example of a landing page situation that should be tested (by someone)! I am not going to name any names here, but in the course of my two decades in the internet marketing business – I have noticed that some of the most ugly, poorly devised web pages have outperformed identically functioning webpages that boast high-quality, high-resolution designs. Whenever I come across one of these "ugly duckling, kick ass websites," I wonder – *How on earth does this happen?*

I have no idea. Sure, I usually have a hunch about what is causing it, but no one knows, really. What would I do if I were running one of these "ugly duckling" sites?

How would I find out what is at the root of our success?

I would run an A/B test and find out how people are reacting differently to the A page (the "ugly" low-tech page) versus the B page (the "pretty" high-tech snazzy page). I would collect a large amount of data on both pages – then analyze the different ways the customers were reacting to both pages. When it comes to web design, people think instinct plays a role. Not really. It's all about the data.

That is what A/B Testing is all about.

You can find several useful tools for A/B testing within *Google Analytics*, as well as with another company called *Optimizely*. Whether it's Optimizely, Google Analytics, or another A/B testing tool out there – it's important to understand that the tests must be setup correctly from a web development standpoint, in order for them to prove anything.

For all of you DIY entrepreneurs, you will be happy to know, it is possible to set these up yourselves (such as adding a goal in Google Analytics) or by placing code on your site (if you know HTML).

But if you want my opinion, let the professionals handle this one.

You've got enough on your plate. Delegate this down to your web developer so they can make sure they have taken all the technical steps to make sure you're A/B test is setup and tracking properly.

Either way you test your site — if you do it right, it will only help your marketing dollars go further, and you will get a better performance from your digital advertising. I have personally tested and tested my landing pages when developing nearly all of my business sites. Sometimes my research proved I knew absolutely nothing about what works better! But other times the testing proved my hypothesis.

If you are still looking for that perfect mix, keep testing your landing page theories with real quantifiable data, to find the right combination of elements that will max out your landing page conversion rate.

Test and quantify then test again. And remember to keep it simple.

That's how the internet was created, and it's what I want you to do with your marketing landing page(s) — so you never lose a big kahuna on the line, and are "optimizing your catch" every day.

STEP TWENTY-THREE:

LEVERAGE SEARCH ENGINE MARKETING

"Search marketing is critically important to online businesses. You can spend every penny you have on a site, but it will be for nothing if nobody knows your site is there."
— *Mark Ostrovsky*

As a young aspiring tech entrepreneur, I absorbed everything I could about a practice called Search Engine Marketing while working at companies like *Ask Jeeves, Yahoo, Amazon*, and attempting to start my own search engine, *SearchChips.com* – which I detailed earlier in the book. As you know, my *SearchChips.com* venture did not turn out so well – but I never gave up trying to use that knowledge to build a winning business around it. If you've never heard of *Search Engine Marketing* (or *Search Marketing*, for short) you really should get to know it right now – because it just might save your business. It saved mine.

There are a lot of moving parts that can go into an effective campaign, but at its essence, Search Marketing *is an online marketing strategy that drives more high-volume, high-quality traffic to your site by increasing the visibility of your business in search engine results.*

Sound great, right? That's because it is. At every stop in my career, I studied the Search Marketing process to see how I could do it better. I will admit it became a little obsession of mine. I spent years taking in what I learned from my years at those big tech firms (some of which were search engine companies) until I was fortunate to partner with my colleague Burt Breznick, who challenged me to use my knowledge to build another search marketing-related business.

Burt was an amazing motivator so once we began brainstorming, the new ideas came fast and furious. Burt and I built our first site: a daily deal aggregator called *Premu.com*, (which was a disappointment). It eventually morphed into *PremuMedia.com*, an internet advertising agency (a big success). Burt and I were extremely pleased that *PremuMedia.com* took off and were able to repay our investment capital – but we weren't satisfied, so we began thinking about how we could create something even more groundbreaking. I still remember how Burt pushed me create something new in the search engine world. Burt left it up to me to actually come up with the idea, thanks Burt! But after brainstorming my brains out, something amazing happened.

One year after Burt laid down the gauntlet, my current company, *SearchMarketers.com* was born. It was the best idea for a web business I'd ever had, so far. For years, it has become my primary business; I believe in it that much. I'm not the only one who believes – in the years since I first conceived the idea for *SearchMarketers.com*, it has become the 4th *fastest growing company in the United States* and #1 *fastest growing marketing company in the USA.*

I knew Search Marketing was an up and coming tech field but I never knew it would be this huge. How did we get here? *Search Marketing is how.* You may also be interested to know *I also followed every step in this book* to build a profitable web business. I'm telling you, I'm not making these steps up out of thin air – so feel heartened. I am leading you down a proven path to success!

Since I have literally built my business around Search Marketing, you can probably imagine that (yes) I really think you should strongly consider using it to promote your internet business.

I can assure you, I'm not just promoting my current company here. Think of it this way: I would never entrust my family's livelihood to it if I did not truly believe in its power to revolutionize a business. *Search marketing can revolutionize your business too, so give it a chance.* How does it work?

SEM versus SEO

Before we start, I can hear some of you asking – "Wait, SEM sounds an awful lot like SEO (Search Engine Optimization), am I right?" Yes, it does – especially when both terms are sometimes used interchangeably by people in the tech world, which can make matters even more confusing. So what is the difference? SEO can be done on its own but it is usually part of a larger Search Engine Marketing campaign.

Yes, virtually every SEM campaign involves SEO, but they also often include other tactics like SSM (Social Media Marketing), the use of *paid search components like pay per click (PPC) or cost per click (CPC) campaigns,* as well as advertisements. This sounds pretty straightforward – so what is the big secret here?

High Volume and High Quality Clients? Yes, Please

There is no big secret. With a name like *SearchMarketers.com,* our "secret sauce" is all about *executing amazingly effective Search Marketing campaigns.* It's that simple. I place Search Marketing far above all other marketing strategies because it's proven to generate tremendous growth revenue in virtually every company I've seen, which uses it properly.

But what's remarkable is, even today, when you can buy entire books on the power of Search Engine Marketing, a lot of really smart people still do not realize its power, which is really strange, if you ask me – but you won't see me complaining about it anytime soon, because it just means more business for me. But, since you and I are friends, let me give you a few inside tips that I would never tell my competition.

The reason I built an entire company around Search Marketing is not just because of the increased traffic it brings (which is really nice), it's *because the traffic driven to your site from search engines is the highest quality traffic you can get on the internet.* And if you are going to advertise on the internet, my theory is – why not focus on getting the best quality traffic you possibly can? Imagine what your best, most sure thing customer would look like – they'd probably be online shoppers, right, since most people shop online these days? So, why not focus solely on attracting the sure things?

This is the target demographic for any good search marketing campaign because *these are the people who are actively seeking out what you offer.* They are searching for products or services just like yours, which means, they want to give you their money! Sales leads don't get much better than that. If you can create a successful search marketing campaign for your own business – I can almost guarantee it will drive more high-quality clients to your front door. And if you are pairing an effective search marketing campaign with a *winning website, powerful landing page,* and a *quality product or service*, I'm telling you, your business is going to flourish for years to come.

Getting Started On Your Own Campaign

Are you sold on giving Search Marketing a shot? Fantastic news. You won't be sorry. I realize you don't have a huge marketing budget so the next question I want to address is – how can you get the most out of your campaign? I'm really glad you asked but I'm not the only Search Marketing expert around. There are a bunch of books out there about Search Marketing, as well as books on how to build a *Google Adwords* campaign (which I will touch on later). So if you want to pull off a professional campaign, I suggest you use Step Twenty-Three as a primer and then go seek out more information. I honestly do not have enough space to give you all the answers. My goal here is to simply provide you with a great foundation of knowledge, as well as some tips for success and some pitfall warnings, so you can understand what an effective search strategy looks like.

Show Some Patience

The first thing you need to understand is you have to *show some patience* when it comes to seeing results. This is the hardest thing for my clients because we live in an instant gratification world – but success does not come overnight. It never does. You have to invest resources and time into a search marketing campaign to really see its value. From my experience, *it can take 3-6 months of continued optimization before getting the results you need.* But if you execute the plan, from that point forward, your web business will likely experience a tremendous influx of consistent high quality traffic for years to come.

Believe me, I spent years trying to punch holes in this theory – and I just can't. This kind of performance is hard to match elsewhere – trust me, I tried! Don't just take my word for it. Some of my previous clients from *Ask Jeeves* have been running their own Search Marketing campaigns for over 20 years. They'd tell you whatever it took to get it up and running was more than worth the investment. So let's get started on yours.

Limit Your Upfront Risk

A lot of my clients like to ask – is Search Marketing foolproof? I always tell them that nothing works like magic, except magic. And as far as I can tell, unless know something I don't, magic does not exist on this planet – so for your Search Marketing campaign to work – you will need more than a magic wand to pull it off. You will need these following elements to all come to fruition in order for it to succeed: *a solid business plan, a great product or service, and a great landing page.* Combine that with a lot of *hard work, tons of optimization,* and a steadfast *commitment to making your campaign a success* – and you will have a winning campaign on your hands.

With a new company just starting out, in order to give yourself time to succeed, you are going to want to *limit your upfront risk,* so you don't run out of money a few months into the campaign. I will say it again: longevity greatly increases your chances of success. If you have all of the key elements I listed above, but don't have the funding to make it happen –

you need to buy yourself time to let the process work its magic, somehow – but how? I suggest you work with a Search Marketing agency (it doesn't have to be my company, I'm not shilling here – but *like mine*) to get your campaign setup. You can often set up a payment system where you pay them a little more on the back end as soon as the new clients start rolling in.

Now if you start seeing results, but happen to run out of money before the big influx of quality clients comes pouring in – you can always take extreme measures, and do what I did by mortgaging your future. I am kidding (sort of), but I did pay for a large portion of *SearchMarketers.com* on credit cards until I finally did see results, which led to me getting more clients, more revenues and yes, eventually higher credit limits!

If racking up credit card debt makes you queasy, it all boils down to how much risk are you willing to take to achieve your dreams? And how much do you believe in the product or service you are selling? If you don't believe, who else will? Don't be afraid to go all in if you truly believe in what you are doing.

That is what I did, and it paid off.

Google Adwords

Now let's get down to the specifics of what an effective search marketing campaign looks like. On a very basic level, every search marketing campaign is built around something called "company sponsored search results" that you already see all the time on Google. Let's say you want to buy a Smart Television and you Google it and start shopping around. But you don't buy one yet. Then later on, you start seeing ads pop up in future Google searches that offer more Smart TVs for you to buy.

Have you ever wondered how those ads got there? It's not magic. The answer is search marketing. Some smart company is paying for those ads to pop up whenever you search for a smart television. You may not even realize you are running a company-sponsored search, but the results you get will be very different from an "organic search result" on the same subject (that is only driven by SEO). How?

The company-sponsored search prominently displays companies who advertise in something called *Google Adwords*. Most people look at this setup as simply a "pay to play" trade-off, which is somewhat true. However, Google Adwords is a lot smarter than that. A company who simply advertises in Google Adwords will not always show up higher in a sponsored Google Search just because it paid more.

When you pay to use Google Adwords, you really are paying for something called a *CPC* or (*Cost Per Click*) – which is a set up where an advertising business (that's you) pays a publisher (in this case, Google) a small fee every time your ad is clicked. You can set your "bid" for how much you would like to pay every time someone clicks on your ad, except Google (not you) will determine the actual price you pay for each ad click in the end. That may sound odd, but that's the way it works.

When you make a bid, Google also measures something called *Quality Score* (which is a rating system, from 1 to 10) for each ad space, or searchable keyword you bid on. No one knows for sure every factor Google uses to calculate Quality Score, however, it's clear the most common factors are *ad relevance, click through rate, landing page quality*, and (of course) your *bid*. So what does all this mean? It means it is still a competition! The best business who advertises on AdWords, will win. Even when you bid high on a CPC in Google AdWords, it does not mean your business will immediately skyrocket to the top of the search results, especially if your *ad relevance, click through rate*, and *landing page quality* are not good.

Conversely, a business that may put in a much lower CPC bid than other competing companies can show up higher in Google search rankings than the company who paid a much higher cost. How the heck can you pull this magic trick off? It takes a really smart business running a really smart Google advertising campaign to succeed. That is usually where my business comes into play – we make smart companies, look a whole lot smarter.

STEP TWENTY-FOUR:

CRUSH IT ON GOOGLE ADVERTISING

"I personally love SEO and think having an SEO plan is a key part to online success. That said, PPC will get you to the top of the search results in minutes."
– John Rampton (Forbes Magazine)

Now that you know a little about how *Google Adwords* work, it's time for you start crushing it on *Google Advertising*. I call this using the *"Grow Grow Trim* strategy" with all of my *SearchMarketer* clients. We have proven this model to be extremely successful so I hope you appreciate the free consultation!

I want to explain the *Grow Grow Trim* strategy further by using an example from the real world. The company I'm going to use is an online retailer called *Beyond the Rack*. The first year after they began to use Search Marketing, their sales hit $6 million. The second year, their sales hit $50 million, and in their third year, they hit $100 million in sales — all because of one ongoing campaign.

How is it possible to have this kind of insane growth? Answer: Search Marketing.

Beyond the Rack is just one of countless companies to follow the *Grow Grow Trim* strategy. Hundreds of our clients have used it like *Groupon, Proactiv, 800Flowers*, as well as many others who are not clients — like virtually every other hyper-fast growing internet based business on earth. It's that popular. Just take a look at *Beyond The Rack's* data I got by taking a screenshot at a high-level meeting at Google headquarters (see illustration below). What's not to like about this?

1. Adopt a Growth Mindset

What is interesting about this graph is that, you can see their customers continue to grow tremendously on the left, while their Cost Per Customer fluctuated (up and down) due to the testing. They didn't give up when Cost Per Customer was high from testing; they continued to optimize. Over time this brought their Cost Per Customer down and continued their massive growth (see right graph).

With all of this data available, I still find it amazing that only a select few really understand the power of Search

Customers Per Week

Average CPA Per Week

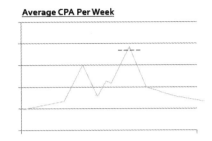

BEYONDTHERACK

"The way to grow is to think about Growth First, efficiency Second and running Tests while giving them enough time to gain learnings"

Marketing. Maybe plenty of others get it, but have some excuse for not following through? Maybe they run out of patience, or time, or money – but there is no denying this strategy works. In my nearly 20 years in the tech industry, I have never seen another form of advertising work like a Search Marketing campaign does on Google. Think about it: Google is our information God. We use it for everything in our lives – so I say – why not use it to market your business? Of the thousands of campaigns I have ran over the years, I have only seen a handful not work like gangbusters, and that was because the advertiser's business was flawed in some way.

Bottom line: it is almost impossible to fail when effectively search marketing a great product or service to Google customers. *So adopt a growth mindset and do it already.* Consider this: Allowing yourself time for testing and optimization will provide you with the data you need to turn your Search Marketing campaign profitable over time. And any lost investment you may end up taking in the early days will eventually be imperative steps you had to take to be successful in the long run.

Now I realize you don't have a ton of resources to throw at this right now, so you must be risk adverse. I also understand why many CEOs will cut and run at the first sign of losses – because they have to! But, this is not a wise move in the long run. From my experience, the advertiser that sticks with Google until it works will win in the end.

2. Maximize Quarterly, Not Daily Results

Just check out the customer growth for *Beyond the Rack* over time. It's amazing. Yes, the cost per acquiring a customer may have fluctuated but over time, but the data is clear as day. Let Google work its form of magic and a good Search Marketing campaign will, over time, allow you to grow within your metrics of success.

I can't tell you how many advertisers look at the daily fluctuations of their campaign performance and make impulsive decisions. This is like making a change to your stock portfolio after every day. Don't do it. You have to be patient. That stock may seem like it's losing money but if you give it time, it goes back up. The same "buy low, sell high" axiom goes for advertising.

Each day will bring different results, but it's important that you look at results from a broader viewpoint, like over a business quarter. That way you can factor in things like seasonality to your performance. I truly believe that if half of your marketing budget is focused on the bottom-line results, and the other half is purely dedicated to testing – how much new business will you find as you go? A lot, if you ask me!

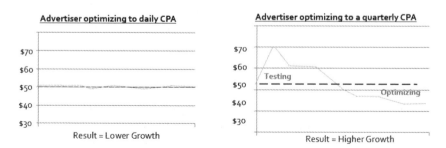

Alternative: Split your budget into a performance budget that has to hit specific metrics + a test Budget to look for new growth

From my experience, the *Grow Grow Trim* strategy will translate to record growth for your business if you just give it some time. So give it some time.

3. Don't Over Optimize

One of the worst mistakes you can make is canceling all the advertising that does not meet your strict performance goals. In order to grow, you must look at your campaign holistically, and work towards an overall goal.

In the above example from *Beyond the Rack*, a shortsighted marketing person might suggest – Hey, *let's cut Display Marketing as its losing money against our Cost Per Action goal.* This move is not wise for many reasons. First, it's not like Display marketing is not driving any new sales – it clearly is driving the most new sales of all your advertising channels, so don't give up on it.

If you continue to do more testing with Display Marketing, you may find it could be optimized below your targets if you give it time to perform. Keep in mind, you should also measure the impact of the people who say, see your Display ad and then do a web search for your business (this is what we call a *view-through conversion*).

When you take all those factors into consideration and look at these figures holistically, guess what – you're looking

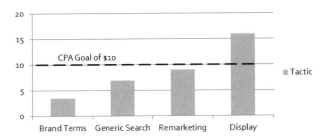

BTR
BEYONDTHERACK

"Having less focus on each specific tactic yet trusting the team in hitting an overall goal has helped us run the right tests to find success."

163

pretty darn good! Your overall CPA (Cost Per Action) goal is being met across all of your tactics and channels, which is allowing your business to stay competitive in the marketplace and continue to grow. Of course, if you're not growing, then you're dying – and if you lose your inventory you could be out of luck down the road. But I say it's the bold advertiser that continues to take chances, experiments, tests, and continues to grow – that will find the new opportunities that allow their business to dominate.

Get Your Match Types Right!

Do you want to know why most new advertisers on Google are unsuccessful? It's because of a simple mistake: they set up incorrect *match types* on their keywords! Check out the InfoGraphic below to get familiar with different match types so you do not make that mistake.

- **Exact Match** – Shows your ad for that exact keyword.
- **Phrase Match** – Shows your ad for any searches with that phrase in it.
- **BMM Modifier** – Shows your ad for any related search in that category.
- **Broad Match** – Matches you to anything Google feels is relevant.

All of these options can work, you just need to bid accordingly, test, and ensure you are using the most relevant keywords. For *Phrase, BMM,* and *Broad Matches,* you can view the details of your actual searches and add something called *negative keywords* so your ad doesn't show up for related searches that aren't relevant.

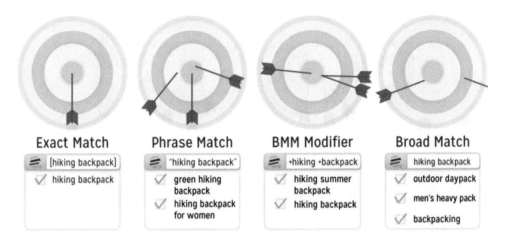

Pitfalls To Avoid

I will leave you with some final common mistakes that can torpedo any good search marketing campaign, be sure to avoid all of these novice mistakes.

- **Geo-Targeting** – Many campaigns are setup with incorrect Geo Targeting, which is a method of determining the location of a visitor to your site, and delivering different content to that visitor based on their location. It's vitally important you have the exact locations in each Google adwords campaign.

- **Device Targeting** – Many advertisers don't have websites properly optimized for Mobile marketing, and incorrectly setup their campaigns. Don't make this mistake. A majority of all web searches are now done on mobile smartphones.

And mobile devices have great conversion rates:

2.60% (higher than desktop!)   2.51%   0.79%

Tips to Optimize for Devices:

TABLET	DESKTOP	MOBILE
(Add %device to destination URLs to adjust or responsive CSS to create a better tablet experience)	Continually A/B test ads & landing page creative vs a control to increase conversion rates and visitor satisfaction, as well as to eliminate guesswork	(Use bid multiplier in Google enhanced campaigns - implement responsive CSS design) Use API Auto-Adjust Bid Multiplier on every bid change

- **Remarketing** – Many campaigns don't leverage remarketing. This is one of the most valuable tools you can use in Google. Remember the Smart TV example? This is remarketing (which is an important factor in any good search marketing campaign). It allows you to position targeted ads in front of a defined audience that had previously visited your website as they browse elsewhere around the internet. It's a great way to connect with visitors who may not have made an immediate purchase.

Your website is visited

A cookie is installed

Return visitors and conversions

Your ads show on the Display Network

- **Google Campaign Ad Extensions** — Finally, so many advertisers don't set up *Google Ad Extensions*. I ask why? Google has added a bunch of different extensions you can easily add-on to your advertisement to take up more real estate in Google, and the more real estate you own, the more likely you are to get eyeballs on it. Check out this graphic below to see a checklist of some popular ad extensions you can add into your Google campaign.

STEP TWENTY-FIVE:

NOW IS YOUR TIME TO TAKE ACTION, DON'T WAIT

"Nothing is anything, until
it is something first."
— *Joe Britton*

I've found that being an internet entrepreneur is a lot like life. You will taste both the sweet and sour, no matter what you do. Yes, it can be an absolute thrill ride when things go as planned, but it can also be tremendously challenging when plans fall apart. If you're like many of the burgeoning web business owners out there, who hang their digital shingles on the web, and expect a magical Brinks Truck to show up and start unloading millions of internet dollars into their PayPal accounts – you will likely experience some growing pains (as reality hits) on your journey toward your ultimate dream.

It's never as easy as that. Nothing ever is. Once your web business is up and running, competitors will try to test your resolve, outsiders will try to burst your bubble – and when things are going great, trouble will always be lurking just over the horizon – so you have to be prepared (mentally, spiritually and emotionally) to weather any storm that comes your way. In other words, this is gut check time. How strong is yours?

I like to tell people who want to start their own internet business that you have to steel yourself before going into the business arena, so you have what I call the "heart for the fight" – which is a term I didn't make up, I actually think I stole that line off of Tupac Shakur – but it really rings true in my world, and I believe it will in yours, too. You don't have to be built like a gladiator to be a champion, but you need to

Get granular with ad group level sitelinks from:

✓ Google Enhanced Campaigns ✓ Social
✓ Call extensions ✓ Location
✓ Product extensions ✓ Checkout
✓ Reviews ...and more

have the heart of one to succeed in this highly competitive business arena.

I don't care what great idea you have, or what corner of the web you're doing business in – it's going to be a street fight among your competition, which can be a lonely proposition because it's a fight you will (largely) have to take on yourself. Even if you hire an army of talented employees, you, as the founder and CEO, will be the only person responsible for the survival of your business. You cannot sit back (like a lot of people who work for big corporations) and passively blame your boss, or the bureaucratic system, for failing you. No, this is all up to *you*.

You can take this news two ways – as a thrilling or terrifying prospect.

I'm telling you all this, here at the end of the book – because I know you may be having mixed feelings, now that you're almost finished reading it. You may be wondering – *Can I really do this? Am I in over my head?*

Trust me, I've felt all of those feelings before. It's totally normal. But rather than staying frozen like a deer in the headlights, I want you to learn how to embrace the pressure of the situation, and become the crunch time performer your business is going to need to thrive when the game is on the line.

I want you to learn how to be the walking, talking illustration of what a clutch performer looks and sounds like in every business interaction you have – because this internet business venture you are about to undertake is not a hobby.

This is your life – so I want you to get your game face on right now.

If you're not exactly the competitive type, that's OK, but you may want to start practicing your game face in the mirror! That is a joke, partially – I realize everyone is different. I'm not saying you have to pop on *Rocky III* and work out to "The Eye of the Tiger" before you go into the office, every day.

But I want you to do whatever it takes to get yourself in the right mental state, so you can stay focused, positive, determined, and most importantly, totally energized to run through all the obstacles that are going to try and get in your way – because there are going to be plenty of them. In my 20 years as an internet entrepreneur, I've found one of the biggest untold secrets to success is – *it will largely be determined (not by what you are selling) but by how well you adapt to the curveballs that will be thrown at you.*

So be smart, be strong, be confident, and be highly adaptable.

The good news for you is – you already have the smarts part covered! In your hands, this very second, is the blueprint you need to make your web business a profitable reality. Now what are you going to do with it?"

Stay Centered And Roll With The Punches

As a man in my 20s, I used to run the gamut of emotions in my business life. I'd get really excited when good things happened like having a big idea, receiving a big award, recruiting an awesome new employee, or signing a new business deal. But I remember, I'd also allow myself to get down about mistakes I made along the way, which did me no good in the long run.

I know this can be difficult to control when the world feels like it's crashing down around you, but I want you to do your best to "stay centered" no matter what life throws at you. *Right in the middle of the road* is where you want to be mentally at all times. It took me quite a few years to realize this, and learn how to roll with the punches.

But I did, and I really hope you will learn that mental skill too, so you let any problems you may encounter flow off you like water on a duck (so to speak).

This is how you will survive, mentally – by staying even, by not sweating the small stuff and by keeping a positive outlook, at all times. There will be always be highs and lows, but if you continue to believe in yourself, focus on what matters, and keep working harder than your competition, you are going to come out victorious in the end.

I like to tell people – *Everything you do, every decision you make for your business is cumulative.* There will be countless decisions you have to make as entrepreneur – *Should I hire this person? Should I get this office? Should I take on this business loan? How much should I spend on advertising?* The questions will keep coming. Don't get hung up on any of them.

Do your best, learn from your mistakes, and move on to the next challenge. It's as simple as that. Because let's face it, we're all human; so in the beginning, you will probably make some mistakes (because we all do). But over time, if you're smart and adaptable, you will get better at making the right decisions. And if you keep fighting the good fight, you will eventually be able to look back at your work from a cumulative perspective – and see that your good decisions greatly outweighed the bad ones.

So don't beat yourself up over the mistakes like I did in my 20s. Just learn from them so that you're always "falling forward," and growing stronger and wiser, no matter what's thrown in your way.

And whatever you do, don't stop moving! You have to keep pressing ahead even when you screw up, while remaining confident in the knowledge that every single minute you put into work, and every task you complete will accumulate over time into something amazing, and your business will grow as a result. It will work. Just give it time.

Remember, Rome wasn't built in a day.

When All Else Fails, Go Forrest Gump On Their Asses

I want to end this by sharing a funny and inspirational story that has nothing to do (directly) with business – but it illustrates what having "the heart for the fight" means to me. I can't show you any tape of my best business deals because they don't exist. But what I can show you is an example of a scrappy individual who may not have been the most talented person in the arena – but he had the biggest will to win – which is my dream for you.

The story happened when I was a teenager – each year, my high school held a ping pong tournament called "May Madness." The tournament was televised on local cable television and I happened to be one of the tournament's top seeds, two years in a row. In the first year, I breezed through the tournament and won, no story there. But my second year, I met the toughest match of my life in the semi-finals.

My opponent knew how to combat my strengths and play to my weaknesses – but I refused to go down. During an epic match (you objectively must see to believe), something literally out of the movie *Forrest Gump* occurred.

There came a time, late in an extremely close match where I served the ball, and what ensued was a ridiculous battle to win one of the best ping pong points of all time. I won't tell you how it ended, but I will say I played most of the point lying on the ground.

What I learned from this experience was, no matter how good you are at something; there will always be someone who is better, so whenever you face a big challenge, or have to do battle with a heavy hitting adversary, you need to conjure your inner Forrest, and find the will to win.

That said, we don't always win in life. So when you give it your all and you still lose – you can hold your head high, knowing that you gave it everything you had.

Here are a few screen shots of the match ...

From the look of these pictures, does it look like I won the point? You have to watch to find out. Just search "Joe Britton Ping Pong Point" for the big reveal. What, do you think I'm going to end on a losing note? LOL.

Now it's your move.

www.GrowGrowTrim.com